RISE ABOVE, BE
Unstoppable!

THE ULTIMATE GROWTH MINDSET FOR TEENS

to Overcome Challenges, Build Resilience, and Prepare for Success

Ariana Smith

ISBN 978-9916-9880-7-7 (eBook)
ISBN 978-9916-9880-6-0 (paperback)
ISBN 978-9916-9880-5-3 (hardcover)

www.ariana-smith.com

CONTENTS

Something For You

Scan the QR code below to get my new books for FREE!

1

DANDELION BOUQUETS

Have you ever picked a dandelion bouquet?

"Never-have-I-ever made a dandelion bouquet." You might not even know what a dandelion is. Well, first of all, a dandelion is a very resilient little yellow flower. A flower with the word 'lion' in it tells us a lot! The puffball of seeds (sometimes called a clock) is often said to make wishes come true when you pick one and blow on it, to scatter the seeds in the wind. A person could take quite a few lessons from the little yellow dandelion flower, and some of those lessons will be found in this book.

Growth spurts

Dandelions are kind of like teenagers. You might be scratching your head and asking right now; *How am I like a dandelion?* It's because the flowers grow so fast, just like you are growing up so quickly. Doesn't everyone tell you that? Parents and grandparents usually look at teenagers and just shake their heads because they can't believe you grow so quickly. Maybe you already look down at the top of your grandma or grandpa's head. In fact, when you are about twelve and thirteen, you can change clothes and shoe sizes in a month, or a matter of weeks! Has your mom or dad griped about you growing out of your shoes and clothes too quickly? Yah, like you can stop eating, right? Of course, you won't stop eating, because you want to grow to the height you are supposed to, and you want to look exactly how you are supposed to look.

What could that be? Absolutely anything you grow up *into* is a 'perfect you.' More on this later, but just know that every human grows into the person they are supposed to be, and with a little bit of personal work, the person they want to be, or to become. In truth, you are a work in progress! No architect of great buildings starts from the top down. In fact, even a three-year-old child building a toy block tower knows that blocks must first be placed on the floor as the *foundation*. Then, and only then, can the block tower grow to new heights.

What is a "growth mindset"?

You will learn in this book how important it is to have a growth mindset. This is your commitment to yourself that throughout your life, you will continue to learn, and your mind will continue to expand with new ideas. Just like the little yellow dandelion, which sends its roots sometimes fifteen feet deep, you will learn how to have a determined growth mindset to make your dreams come true. This means that throughout your life you will continually keep an open mind, so as to learn about new things, learn new approaches to old problems, and to new problems too. You will not allow your thought process to stagnate and become fixed with an unchanging mindset.

Your roots will also grow deep and strong like those of the dandelion, with a deep-rooted education, your well-thought-out plans, bountiful dreams, and goals as your guide. You will begin to see how your growth mindset is always open to change and to actual growth. Perhaps that is where the ancient saying about having a *small mind* came from. Your mind must be ready and eager to embrace all the wonderful changes which are ahead of you in your life! A mind needs to grow! A fixed mindset works great for some things, like working hard and always doing your best, but a fixed mindset in other aspects of life might hold you back from exploring new avenues.

For example, if you say, "I hate science. I will never like science! I will avoid anything that has to do with science," your fixed mindset will keep you from exploring all the many different fields of science which you might enjoy and like. Having a fixed mindset with some things in your life can put limitations on your opportunities.

A growth mindset is always open to new possibilities, new challenges, and new ways of looking at ideas, problems, and issues. Perhaps for a teenager, learning and knowing when to have a fixed mindset and a growth mindset is a worthy goal. Just like the dandelion, a teenager's goal is to be a survivor and thrive.

What characteristics about teens and dandelions are similar?

Dandelions spread out and send down their roots deep into the soil for their firm foundation. Whoa, they grow deep, right? The dandelions know that when their roots are strong and deep, they have a firm foundation. Even when the lawn mower cuts off their tops, within days they grow a new flower, and spread out even further. Teenagers also like to spread out. Some teenagers are said to be "deep"—meaning they are deep-thinkers who consider things carefully before acting. Channeling your deep thoughts, dreams, and wishes into productive *ACTION* is why you are reading this book!

Clones?

A dandelion can also clone itself if its root is cut, something which, so far, humans don't know how to do. That isn't saying we won't know how to do that sort of cloning someday in the future. In fact, in truth, parts of people's bodies can be cloned right now. In some places in the world scientists actually are cloning embryos by extracting stem cells (which can produce either more stem cells or "specialist" cells that grow into specific organs) from the blastocyst (a structure made of cells in mammals that actually forms the embryo in a later stage of development) and telling the cells which organ they need to produce. But that's a discussion for another time about science and human ethics.[1] It is just important to know how resilient a dandelion can be and how you would do well to imitate that resiliency!

Yes, for now, you can think of yourself as being like a bright yellow dandelion. Nothing can stop you from growing and maturing, following your own purpose, and pursuing your dreams in this world.

The warmth of sunshine

Here's the sad part about the dandelion. A dandelion cannot grow without sunlight. In many ways, you also need *sunlight,* not only in the form of true, warm, bright sunlight rays, but also you need to receive the warmth and good feelings when someone cares, and loves, and nurtures you.

The thing is, even IF you are not being lovingly nurtured, you must learn to nurture yourself! You will be with "you" your entire life—who better than you to make sure you have what you need in this world? You must be resilient like the dandelion.

The human connection

A dandelion does not need other dandelions. A dandelion doesn't even need bee pollination to continue its species. It develops "apomictically"—meaning on its own. That little yellow flower has no need of any other dandelions to ensure its success and happiness. However, the fact remains, humans need other humans, and they need human contact. After all, you are not a dandelion. If humans do not get the love and the touch they need, they can become *touch starved*. This negative feeling is also known as *touch deprivation*. This lack of human love or proper nurturing can cause some infants to develop a condition called *failure to thrive*, meaning they are small and underweight for their age and develop more slowly than normal. This condition may result in problems for teenagers in their teen years.

Fear of abandonment

The teen years are full of so many challenges. It is difficult to negotiate all the challenges by oneself, and yet, many teenagers find themselves feeling like they are all alone. After all, teens are entering the age when they want to know that their parents won't abandon them, no matter what they do or how they behave. Teenagers, and people in general, need unconditional love.

Back-off mentality!

However, many teenagers don't like other people touching them. After all, this is a time when a teenager begins to feel their independence. However, "Failing to experience frequent positive touch as a child may affect the development of the child's and social skills—although this isn't true for everyone."[2] It could also hamper a person's ability to focus and learn.

Why do humans have this problem?

Many humans do not get the loving touch of a hug or a pat on the back. In fact, A LOT of humans don't receive the nurturing they need. The lack of touch creates *touch deprivation,* which can affect a person throughout their childhood, their teens, and beyond, into their adult lives. *How do you get hugs from your family if they are not a "huggy" type* of family? It is easy to just say, "Give *them* hugs," but it is the truth; some parents aren't huggers. Some parents don't know how to nurture their children, perhaps through no fault of their own. Many parents are just so preoccupied with their own life struggles that they do not recognize the touch deprivation they have created in their own offspring.

Hugs and affection have to start somewhere, like that song about peace in the world where it says, "Let there be peace on earth and let it begin with me." [3] If you start hugging the person you want a reciprocal hug from, chances are they will soon be hugging you back.

Even if you say, "I am not touch starved," the chances are you might be.

What are the signs of being 'touch starved'?

- You might have a sense of being depressed

- You might have a general feeling of anxiety

- You might have a general, overall stressed feeling

- You might not be very happy in any of your relationships/friendships

- You might not be able to sleep, or you may sleep too much

- You might prefer to not have attachments to other people

- You might just push your parents/caregivers/friends away by your negative behavior, intentionally

You are not alone in identifying that you are seeking love, touch, caring, and friendship.

Knowing that you are not alone sometimes helps some people, but not all people. Songs like Stacey Ryan and Ziva Magnolya singing *Fall in Love Alone* [4] are 'reaching out' songs—people *reaching out* for love, for support, and for caring. Often, when a troubled teen listens to this type of song, they identify with the words. Needing touch in your life, mental and physical touch, is a very real necessity to being a healthy, happy person.

Junk food is not a touch starvation solution

Okay, so now you know you might need to take care of your own *touch starvation*. How do you do that? It is not as if you can just eat a gigantic cheeseburger and your need for other human touch will vanish. This is sometimes how obesity begins—when that cheeseburger you eat every day becomes your *best friend*. It is warm, and fulfilling, well, filling anyhow, and for a few moments, you are loving it, and in some warped way, it is loving you. *Isn't there a reference to love in one of those hamburger commercials on TV?* Of course, advertisers know that everyone seeks love and friendship. So, the commercials created by advertisers are selling *hamburger love* and *French fry love* and *candy bar love* and *taco love*. Be aware that many of those commercials on TV, YouTube, and anywhere else, <u>do</u> specifically target the teenager population. Now, you can see how that hamburger becomes *comfort food*. But where can a teenager find the love and care they need to succeed in achieving their dreams and goals? Hint: It is not in a lunch sack or the drive-through.

Word of caution

Word of caution here; beware of *comfort food*. Generally speaking, comfort food isn't a true friend—it comes with consequences later, such as unwanted weight gain, nutritional issues, and clogged arteries from eating too much fat. If you find yourself utilizing "food" as your best "friend" or "go-to" for comfort, it would be wise to seek counseling, and read on and find other ways to help!

What can you do to help with touch starvation?

First of all, what NOT to do!

Sometimes touch-starved teenagers seek out romantic attachments to fill this void in their lives. The problem with this is that any *loving touch* must be made with *genuine, sincere love attached—if not love, at least real 'like' and caring.* Superficial attachment just to get a hug—or more—will not take care of your touch starvation. In fact, it could make it worse and more complicated.

Rejection can be a real stumbling block to achieving success and happiness in your life. Physical satisfaction has a time and a place in your life when you are ready and mature enough. But adding physical satisfaction at a time when all you truly need is a *hug* just might complicate your life and create even more touch deficiency when your chosen partner or you begin to pull away or reject affection which is not given unconditionally. Emotions are not toys to be *played with*—especially YOUR emotions. Truthfully, isn't there enough going on in a teenager's wild and wooly world without adding this type of drama? Just something to think about . . .

Where to seek loving support

First, try very hard to break down the wall you have erected between your parents/caregivers and yourself. Yes, they may act like gatekeepers sometimes, and yes, you may find them quite annoying at times, but they *do* love you. They want the best life for you. Sometimes, it may seem like all they want to do is control you. It is difficult to see their perspective. This is when you might say to them, "I can't wait until I am out of here and can do what I want!" or "You just want to control me!" You want to spread your wings and fly. *Who can blame you for that normal feeling?* No one.

Ways to show and develop your independence

- Take a part-time job after school or on weekends

- You may have a driver's license, but learn to use public transportation—that way, when you need to go somewhere, you can, without using the family car

- Develop a budget of the money you make and your allowance. Begin to save toward a modest goal

- Practice self-regulation of your emotions, learn to "talk" rather than explode or sulk

See your life from a different angle

Perhaps they are desperately in need of a hug—from you. *Did you ever consider that possibility?* Contrary to what most teenagers might believe, parents and caregivers are people, too, just like you! Chances are, if you reach out to hug them, they will hug you back. Especially since the Pandemic, there are a lot of people who are still struggling with *touch starvation.*

Boundaries

It is also important at this point to remind you of *body boundaries.* Some teens get confused and trust people who they should not trust, and touch becomes *bad touch.* You instinctively know what is good and what is bad touch. If the line is blurry to you, speak with your parents, the school nurse, or your doctor, to get help defining what are *healthy love and touch boundaries.* It is very important for a teenager to know the difference.

Drawing a line

Maybe touch is just not your *thing* anyway, so all of this is running in one ear and out the other, so of speak, but being 'touch starved' is not a good thing for any human being. That's why hugs were invented, and high fives, and handshaking, and pats on the back and head, and cheek kissing. Not to generalize too much, but the French have the least problem with *touch starvation.* One could argue that it is all that kissing on each cheek when people greet each other which takes care of their *touch needs.* The English generally keep their distance from each other, sometimes giving them the label of being *cold* which comes from their stand-offish-attitude. The Inuit rub noses and the upper lip for their greetings. Since the Inuit have to keep their bodies completely covered due to the low dangerous temperatures, only their noses and eyes are exposed, but rather than being *touch starved,* they figured out how to rub noses. Genius, right? *Would rubbing noses work for you?* Just asking . . .

So, what can you do?

It's not like you are going to run out and grab someone out on the sidewalk and say, "You look like you need a hug, and so do I!" and just commence hugging! If you do that, well, it could spell trouble. Here's another choice: Animals are great stand-ins for people-hugs. Animals feel so fluffy and warm. *Can you grab a cat or a dog?* Sometimes, even if you don't have your own pet, there might be a stray cat in the neighborhood who will become your friend. Most cats love to be pet, but be careful. Cats do have very sharp claws. Street cats can and do have diseases. Maybe you should pet your neighbor's cat? Perhaps volunteer at the local animal shelter to spend time with a dog or cat; they often need walkers for dogs. Patting an animal often brings good feelings to a person. This is why organizations started taking dogs into hospitals to visit people, and why old people's homes let them have pets or at least pet *visitors*. Animals can be the *stand-ins* for a needed hug and that's a perfectly *good* thing. There are some teenagers who love their pet snake or their pet gerbil. *Do you have a stand-in for your needed hugs?*

Getting outside of yourself

When you care for someone or something outside of yourself, you begin to feel better about yourself. You create a *mindset* of caring for others. People who volunteer at food banks or other outside sources which help others, not only help others, but they also help themselves, as well. When you can show empathy for the plight of others, you are a positive force in the universe. That sounds a bit like something from the galaxies beyond, however, when you think positively, the world around you can become more positive, as well. A positive attitude, especially under adversity, can really make a difference in your life. A positive mindset can and does bring positive results.

- Try not to fear the put-downs of others—be firm in your *mindset*

- Believe your opinions are important and that they matter

- It's okay to express feelings and emotions—when not accomplished in a disruptive manner

• Be conscious of the feelings of others

What is empathy?

Empathy means that you have the mental ability to *walk in someone else's shoes*—to try to understand how that person is feeling. You are not aloof from their sadness, happiness, or confusion. In essence, you *get them*. The equivalent might be "I see you; I hear you." When you have empathy, you *feel* for your friend or family member. You do not say, "You shouldn't feel this way," but instead, you say, "You go ahead and feel what you are feeling, I am here for you."[5]

For you to have true empathy for someone takes courage and commitment. In today's world, as a general rule of thumb, people tend to not want to get involved with other people's lives. This is what contributes to touch deprivation in the first place. "Touch" doesn't just involve a skin-to-skin connection, like a pat on the back, it requires a mind-to-mind connection. In essence, you want to share thoughts with someone and have a mind-to-mind 'hug.'

What is sympathy?

Empathy is quite different from sympathy. Sympathy is when you understand someone's situation, but you keep your distance. You do not get involved in the other individual's ups or downs; you distance yourself from what they are experiencing or thinking. Basically, you do not *get into their business*, or you *mind your own business*.

So, how do you plan to get your touch needs met?

Truthfully, it might take a little planning. Maybe you can squeeze your friend's shoulders, or a fist bump might suffice. Figure out what feels comfortable for you and do it to end your touch starvation!

A game to help with touch starvation is Twister or another one called Doctor! Doctor! For these games to work, of course, you need to have other people to play the games with.

Game of Twister™

Twister™ is a floor game made by Hasbro. You need at least two players. It is fun and truly challenging. When your right hand is on yellow and your left foot on green and your left hand on blue and your right foot on red, you might just tumble or must move over your friend's legs or back! (See where touch starvation gets zapped here?) The downside is that you have to purchase the game and it is around fifteen dollars. You can play with family, friends, or even strangers who will soon be friends! No more *touch starvation* for anyone! That's a very good thing!

Game of Doctor! Doctor!

This game needs no boards, and you don't have to purchase a thing, but you do have to have at least four players, preferably five, because one person has to go hide their eyes while the others get all tied up in knots. *How do they get tied up in knots?* Good question. They form a circle, holding hands, (see, no more touch starvation). Then, they go under each other's arms, or climb over each other's arms, or twirl under each other's arms, over and over until they can't knot themselves up anymore. They cannot let go of holding hands. Then, they call out "Doctor! Doctor!" and the player who has been hiding their eyes must come and point to each one and say things like, "You climb over this arm," and they might hear the group say, "Ow, ow, I can't," because it is not easy to untangle. If any hands break apart when the doctor makes them climb over or under or move, the Doctor must go back to the *office* and the group tangles again. The larger the group, the more difficult the game becomes. No one dare leave still feeling touch deprivation!

No friends around, no family around—just *solo mio?*

Here are some solo suggestions to find neutral touch:[6]

- Get a massage—people who receive massages have more white blood cells to fight sickness; they have less stress cortisol hormone in their blood.

- Get your nails done. Pedi/Mani. This is a gender-neutral attack on needing touch AND feeling and looking better at the same time. Everyone loves a win-win!

- Get your hair cut or styled. Just like getting your nails done, getting your hair coiffed is another way to squeeze in the touch while feeling better about how you look.

- Go to a dance at school or learn a new dance. Sometimes, it costs money to take dance lessons, so you might have to save up, but it can be really fun not only to learn something new, but to *charm* your dance partner at the next school dance. (And yes, touching is required.)

- Connect with your friends, pat their back, hug when you see them. From the outside, watching teenagers huddle and wrap their arms around each other's shoulders might seem oddly *tribal*—and that is exactly what it is. Teenagers DO belong to their own *tribe*. They have their own rituals, their own language, and ultimately, chiefs or leaders do emerge. Hugging is a very real part of some teen groups' bonding.

And, uh, should there be an explanation as to why you are doing all these things, again?

It's scientific! Touch deprived humans don't get enough of the hug hormone, oxytocin. When someone hugs you, this oxytocin hormone is released into your body—and wah-lah! You feel loved and connected. The more you hug, the closer you will feel to your family or your friends. The premise is that unless you *feel wanted, loved, and cared for*, it will be more difficult for you to pursue your goals and dreams. Not impossible, just more difficult . . .

Now let's get back to the dandelion for a moment.

Comic Cheesy Relief: *Just so you know—a cheetah is faster d'an-de-lion. But pound for pound, a dandelion might be stronger* . . .

Obviously, hugging a dandelion isn't going to do much for you, or for anyone else, though taking a walk and picking dandelions might lift your spirits. Maybe holding an armful of dandelions might help, but probably not.

Listen to music. Songs by artists like Ed Sheeran, One Direction, Adele, and Halsey's "Thinking Out Loud" are often comforting. One line in the song called "Your Soul is Evergreen" has such beautiful, truthful words about each and everyone's soul. But of course, you must nurture yourself to keep that soul "evergreen and healthy."

Just a little fantasy. . .

You may not choose to believe it, but *some people say* that those puffballs of dandelion seeds *are* magical. Supposedly, if you pick one puffball and blow on it while making a wish, your wish will come true. *How much would it hurt to try, right?* If you are smiling now, that's a very good thing! Keep smiling and keep reading!

Developing dandelion resilience

This book is going to supply you with solid ideas on how to *thrive* and break through any barriers that might be impeding your success and happiness, but a little *wishing* can't hurt. Just like the dandelion, you can learn to be more resilient to help enable you to achieve the success in life you desire, and ultimately, enhance your personal happiness.

Take note

Just a quick comment here, which you should take note of; *no one in the entire human population of the world is happy all the time.* The sooner you internalize *that* reality, the easier it will be for you to become more resilient. Resilient people love to be happy, yet they do know that, sometimes, happiness can be a bit fleeting, like an elusive butterfly. *Have you ever tried to catch a butterfly?* They ARE quite elusive . . .

Life is a mix of happiness and a little sadness sometimes, and a little disappointment sometimes, too.

Can you imagine if you were euphoric constantly? It would be exhausting!

About Grandma's "Yarn Time"

Before introducing you to *Grandma's Yarn Time,* this is the part of this book where teenagers hear a story about the experiences of another teenager, but first, you need to know what a *yarn* is. A *yarn* can be a story, and sometimes it is an exaggeration of a story, as in saying, *'spin a yarn.'* The word 'yarn' probably originates from the fact that yarn from cotton was formed by making long continuous strands of thread, or fibers *threaded together.* A yarn is a story with the parts of the story all woven together for you to make sense of them. This book will be telling Grandma yarns, here and there.

Grandma's "Yarn Time"

A Teenager's Dandelion Story:

There was once a thirteen-year-old teenager whose mother never let her do the things other girls were doing. *Why?* Perhaps her mother was fearful that something would happen to her daughter when she was away from her. For example, the teenager wanted to go away to night camp for the summer, but her mother would not allow it to happen. Finally, the mother allowed the thirteen-year-old to go to *day camp* on the bus. Most of the children were much younger than the teenage girl, but she was still VERY excited and happy that she got to go on the day camp trip every day for a whole week.

Every day for an entire week the teenager got to be away from her home, and her mother's watchful eyes. Every day she went hiking and swimming in the creek and made outdoor projects. One project was picking something from the outdoors to put behind glass in a picture frame that the campers designed themselves. (Nowadays, putting together glass, a cardboard backing, and rubber-taped picture edges would not be such a *big* deal, but for the teenager it was a big deal!) She had to pick what she would put behind the glass. She had to pick the color of the tape which became the trim. She picked royal blue. *Can you believe she chose a dandelion just forming a fluff of seeds to put behind the glass?* Some of the seeds were already floating off, like tiny white feathers.

To make this long yarn a little shorter, the teenager gave the glass-framed dandelion to her mother at the end of her wonderful week at camp. The only week away at a summer camp the teenager would ever experience in her entire life. Her mother hung the framed dandelion near the stove in the kitchen. Within a week, the resilient seeds pushed and shoved, and popped off the glass, and scattered the dandelion's white fluffy seeds all over the mother's kitchen! *Did the teenager remember to make a wish?* Let's hope so.

The moral of the story? Strength and resilience make things happen, despite any obstacles. That resilient dandelion knew those seeds had to fly away, and the dandelion made it happen.

When you want something or need something, are you resilient, and do you make it happen?

If you always remember the power of the dandelion popping open the picture frame to let its seeds go free, you will remember how important it is that when you are faced with adversity and difficult times in your life, you can persevere—just like the dandelion. Sometimes, you may feel as if you need a bouquet of dandelion fluff to wish upon when life becomes more difficult than usual. (To tell you the truth, you could go pick as many seeding dandelions as you want off of park lawns and probably no one will care.) Wishing hurts no one, right?

How do you know if you are building the resilience within you, like the resilience of a dandelion?

Here are some *dandelion strength identifiers*. There will be more tools for coping offered later on in the book, but for now, understand that you can identify how to be more resilient in your life. Resiliency is like a rubber band snapping back to its original size after being stretched out.

Sometimes, humans get *stretched out* with life's happenings, good ones, and bad ones, yet perseverance and resiliency snap humans back to their original calm selves.

Dandelions don't get washed away

Dandelions put down their deep roots so that wind and rainwater cannot wash them away. A dandelion has such a *mindset* that it even adapted to its roots being split, by growing and cloning itself from the split root. One could say that those teenagers who have experienced their parents getting a divorce are like the dandelions who have learned to split their roots in order to survive and thrive within two households. Teens often must learn to cope with families which have become split, but just like the thriving dandelion, most teens thrive and eventually bloom again, especially when they understand and have their own *mindset* to succeed, no matter what occurs around them. Do you have a *mindset of success*?

Weed comparison—do not snicker and giggle here—a weed is an unwanted plant in a garden)

If you are saying to yourself, *A dandelion is a weed!* Well, yes, *technically*, Taraxacum officinale IS a weed, but it is also a pretty flower that can hold up mountainsides during a downpour of rain. *How many little flowers do you know that can do that?* It has also been used by lovers for centuries for reciting the words "loves me, loves me not," while someone pulls off each of the yellow petals until the last one identifies if one is loved or not. Supposedly, many a love match has ended with a "loves me not" throughout the centuries.

You are a survivor

Humans do need to *feel loved,* don't they? Well, actually a person *could* survive without love IF they loved themselves. If that person took care of themselves and nurtured their own dreams and desires, they would *feel* love, *wouldn't they?* That might be a point to ponder or discuss. *Would loving oneself be enough?* For some teenagers it must be. Some teenagers must learn to nurture themselves into adulthood. So, to begin to build the resilience of a dandelion, start with these steps:

 You begin to think and see yourself as a Survivor. You are **not** a victim. In life there are victims, of course. Victims of violence. Victims of car wrecks.

Victims of disease. Those are all immense tragedies that

perhaps warrant a person feeling like a victim. *Are you a victim involved in any of those happenings?*

If not, you really can't *play* that role in your life, now, can you?

Not with any legitimacy, anyhow. Yes, you may have had difficult obstacles put into your life, like great big boulders trying to stop you or impede your progress toward your goals. A resilient dandelion would grow under that boulder, or over it, or perhaps eventually move that boulder aside with its strong roots.

You can overcome obstacles in life which are put in your path. Yes, life sometimes is not easy, but just like a dandelion, which is stepped on by a heavy boot, it eventually bounces back up. That's resiliency! Say and repeat often: I am a survivor! Sometimes, you may hurt or be disappointed or even disillusioned by others, but you are not a victim. You have the *mindset* of a survivor! You thrive!

Be a bouncing-back-up dandelion! Make up your mind that's who you want to be. You will not always be able to avoid the obstacles in your life, but you can control how you respond to working through the obstacles, and how you view yourself while you deal with them. You are a Survivor!

You begin to identify and to regulate your emotions. Emotions can be sneaky. Sometimes you may not even know WHAT you are feeling. Screaming, crying, sulking, lashing out—*what do you feel?* You may need to just pause, take a breath, and figure out, *what am I feeling? Is it fear? Is it anger? Am I frustrated? Am I hungry?* This means that when you feel sad about something, understand *why* you are feeling sad. Did someone you care about die? Of course, being sad is a normal emotion when you have lost someone you cared about, even a pet like a dog, cat, or gerbil. However, if you wake up sad every single day, it is time for you to make an appointment with a mental health provider who can help you untangle your emotions so that you will know and understand *what is making you sad.* Perhaps too much singular focus has fatigued you into sadness—like too much concentrated Internet time. Just sayin' . . .

If you are angry, identify what is making you angry or upset. Realize that moment of anger *too will pass.* Anger can sometimes make someone become impulsive—and impulses often need to be slowed down. You may *feel* like punching that 'so and so' in the nose, but literally take a step back, breathe deeply, and try to remember your dandelion *status.* Remember the *mindset* you have chosen to maintain. *Do you need a bike ride? Should you run around the block? Hot shower? Cold shower?* What pre-planned ideas have you designed to walk you back from anger when it happens? Take a moment to figure it out.

A new thought process must be nurtured. *When you are angry, do you picture yourself rowing on a lake or swimming in a cool pool?* Generally, deep breathing, a walk around a park, or staring out of a window at a tree in the wind, or birds on the branches, will help pacify your quick anger. Some people count to ten. Imagery is often a way to summon quieter thoughts. *Who can stay angry when picturing a bubbling brook in their mind's eye?* A squishy ball in a top desk drawer often can be utilized for a quick release of that fast, emotional anger. Squish and squeeze—two very handy words when combined with repeated squish and squeeze action on a squishy ball.

5) You take control of your own life. Yes, you are still a teen, and yes, you are subject to parents', caregivers', and teachers' rules and regulations. However, you can steer yourself away from difficult or bad situations. You don't have to add fuel to your own fire. (More later in the book on how teens do this sometimes without realizing it.)

6) You make up your own mind, creating your own *mindset*, to have domain over yourself and your choices. In other words, if all the fish in the school swim left and you *know* there is danger in swimming left because you saw the shadow of a shark, then, you do NOT swim left. You have domain over yourself. You control you. Trust yourself. You might warn the other fish in the school, but you make up your own mind as to what is right for you. You create your own *mindset* ahead of a tragedy. You know your own mindset and you do not even have to stop and think about it. Your *mindset* becomes just that—a "mind" set to do what you want it to do. That's what the teen years are about—sometimes, tough decisions are made, and you end up swimming alone, but usually only for a little while. Your mindset must be to do what is best for YOU and your future and continued success.

Grandma's "Yarn Time"

Once upon a time, a long time ago, you know, when bell-bottom pants were in, and a singing group called the Beatles was famous, there was a teenager who, basically, had a mindset about most things. It was tough holding her ground, but this one time she almost caved. She belonged to the drama class after school group. Every night, they rehearsed a play, MacBeth by Shakespeare. The girl was one of the witches who

stir the cauldron and say, "Cauldron boil, cauldron bubble . . ."
Anyhow, all the drama kids would stay until about ten at night,
even on school nights. It was quite a big privilege they had
in those days. But this time, all the group decided they were
going to pile into the cars of the kids who had their driver's
licenses, and they were not going to rehearse. They were going
to go to the beach and have a gigantic bonfire.

The teenage girl wanted to go. She wanted to go SO badly,
and she probably can still hear them yelling at her calling her
"Goodie Two Shoes" for following her parents' rules. But what
they didn't know was that those rules were her own rules. Her
parents never told her she couldn't do things like that. She
actually chose not to do them!

Anyhow, long yarn cut short, the drama kids decided to drive
their cars onto the beach, and they all got stuck, and they had
to call their parents to come get them, and they had to have
their cars towed out of the sand with tow trucks.

Meanwhile, the next day, the girl listened to their horror
story, but she didn't say anything. Most of her friends were
grounded by their parents. For this teen girl, it wasn't about
the punishment, it was about the trust bond she had with her
parents. *How could parents trust their kids if they went somewhere
other than where they said they would be?*

The teenager was one of those polite types who would not rub
things in people's noses, so she said nothing to her friends who
went to the beach, but she knew she would never forget. If it
had been in today's society, the drama group probably would
have labeled her with nasty names on social media for not
going along, and she might have retaliated with laughing at
them for getting stuck in the sand. In those days things were
easily forgotten, but in today's society, where teens use social

media for at least eight hours per day, that type of encounter can last to "infinity and beyond" (to quote Buzz Lightyear).

Moral of the story: You have your own *mindset.* You are your own boss. You have control of your choices. You are mature enough to do what is right, and to avoid what is wrong. If you have to learn by consequence, that might be just how you learn, sometimes with negative consequences. We all have our own learning styles. The Grandma Yarn finds it is best to think *BEFORE you* make a choice which may not be a good one. Choice is a wonderful thing, but it comes with responsibility and consequences.

Another "Grandma Yarn!"

I know you are just jumpin' for lizards to hear another yarn. This one is about a young man who was home schooled until his senior year in high school. Who knows how his peers viewed him when he entered that school? As a teenager, you would know better how newbies coming through the high school door as a senior might look or feel or be treated. When it came to high school, he was *green,* which meant he didn't know the lingo, the culture, the people. He wouldn't have known how to prepare for the high school 'splash down.'

The thing is, he didn't know, and he couldn't know, and for him, it was major culture shock. *What is culture shock and what can culture shock do?* In this teenager's situation, it turned his life for the worse. He fell into severe depression and loneliness. He had no friends. A doctor might even say he experienced psychosis, as he was moved from the cozy warmth of his home schooling to the harsh reality of a new, confusing, unpleasant high school campus.

Currently, this young man is finishing off seven years in a federal prison for involvement with illicit drugs.

If that comment washed over you like ice water, it was meant to . . .

How can other teenagers who are experiencing culture shock—which can be just from entering high school from a little school—survive? Or how do they survive the reality that says, "Wow, this is it. I am supposed to grow up in the next four years."

This young man did not have the tools to cope with the changes in his life. Yes, it was ice water to him, too. He did not have a friend at the school to confide in and share his fears with. He was too embarrassed to seek out a counselor. He turned to self-medication, self-destruction, and that's how he ended up where he is. Of course, not every teen will plunge this far into destruction, but it is important to be aware.

What can you do to avoid culture shock or any other shocks which might present themselves in your life?

Change is a fact of life. No one can avoid change, and sometimes, change is a good thing.

Nothing ever stays the same, even when we want it to.

There is no such thing as the *status quo.* Change is inevitable.

How can you prepare to keep yourself *psychologically safe* for the changes that are bound to come into your life?

1 Prepare yourself for change if you are given ample time.[7] Some people might call this the "warm up" time. It is when you do the self-talk that "everything is going to be fine," and "you can do this," and "you got this!" In the case of the young man in the Grandma Yarn, there was no time for the young boy to prepare for the change in attending this new high school. His mother announced one summer's day that she was no longer going to home school her five children. She was getting a divorce, a new job, they were moving to a new town, and a new life, in that order, and her children would just have to "learn to cope." Obviously, none of the children had the skillset to cope, but some of them hobbled along, and four of them made it through. One of the girls became much more sullen than the others, and continues to be sullen to this very moment, rarely laughing and experiencing joy. And of course, the young teenage boy is still in prison. The five children could not prepare to have *resilient mindsets*. Only a resilient mindset with a *survivor's mentality* (and a dandelion's strength) could get anyone through so many changes.

2 It is important to build your resilience **PRIOR** to change. This may mean that you investigate everything about the change you are going to experience. If it is a new residence, where is the park, the gym, the library, the swimming pool? How will you get to the school? Are there teen clubs you could join to make new friends?

3 Clarify the reasons for the change. Is it a temporary change? A long-term change? You may have to write the reasons for the change on a piece of paper. Once you understand the reasons behind the change, you are more apt to accept the change and be able to plan.

 What are the "ground rules" for this change? What can or can't you do as a result of these changes?

 Investigate how you can emerge as a survivor through these changes.

Now, back to lessons on becoming a survivor. Yes, making sound, good decisions means you are caring for yourself, you are protecting yourself, and you are always weighing options and consequences. The changes will come in your life, but many of the changes that pop up in your way, you will be able to deal with.

Working through changes

Solve issues or situations around you which you *can* control. *Are you getting a low grade in grammar or science? Would more studying help? Or perhaps having a tutor would help you.* No time to clean your room? *Would having more hooks and boxes to store things help?* If you took an inventory of your room, would there be items you could get rid of which are causing clutter? Visual clutter can oftentimes make mental clutter for some people. *Clean room, clear mind. Did you ever think of cleaning your room for that reason?* The Internet seems to have answers for everything and everyone! Even for how to keep your room clean and clutter-free.

Uncluttered room = uncluttered mind

Room cleaning steps:

1. Pick up all the trash—and that includes the trash under the bed. No, you will NOT use that straw again. Out it goes. After you pick up all the trash, take it to the large family trash can. Re-line the bucket and bring it back to your room.

2. Do the "sniff" test for your clothes, especially if you have mixed clean clothes with dirty clothes.

3. Put all the dirty clothes in the dirty clothes hamper. If you do your own wash, which you *should* be doing at your age, put a load in the machine and get it going. If you want to mix it all together, that's fine if you utilize cold water cycles only.

4. Take all the sheets and pillowcases off your bed and pile them on the floor to go next into the washer.

5. Tackle your dresser top, your desktop, and any other furniture tops covered with "stuff."

6. Dust and wipe down surfaces. That includes lampshades and windowsills.

7. Shine up any mirrors with mirror cleaner, or water and an old newspaper to wipe it off works well.

Love yourself. Sometimes it is difficult to put yourself first and love yourself, but loving yourself means that you will be more easily be able to love others around you. Also, it means respecting yourself, and not letting others belittle or put you down.

If you find that social media is invading your *mental peace of mind,* only you can turn social media off or limit access for yourself. Turning off social media or restricting your own time on social media sounds easier said than done. You may not believe it now, but you will after you try to curtail some of your use. Social media is, unfortunately, very addictive. It is right up there with chocolate, soda, and sugary foods. But here's a word to the wise: restricting yourself can be accomplished. You can have a *mindset* to control your social media use. Set a timer for how long you will allow yourself on social media, phone calls, or game time.

Sometimes, just going outside to *catch the proverbial elusive butterfly* is much better than staring at a computer screen. Self-talk can help you. Tell yourself, out loud if it helps, "I am going to be all right," or "I'm going to be okay" just like in the Lizzo song about "Pressure." The song does have a small word in it that makes it PG, but Lizzo repeats 'turn up the music' and "I'm gonna be all right." (Check with parents first before listening to the song, but it is uplifting). Sometimes, listening to upbeat music helps you get through difficult times. Choose your music wisely. Don't listen to music which might do the opposite of what you hope it will do for you.

You learn to know when to ask for help. It is not an embarrassment to ask for help; it is quite the opposite. *Why wait until you fall further and further behind?* Take care of *you.* Ask for help when you need help. Also, helping others is important, too. When we have empathy for others, we also get the benefits of good hormones surging through our own veins. *Did you know that your brain enjoys those hormones?* They are called endorphins, wand your body makes them to help you feel happy.

2

MEDIA PRESSURE

Is there a real world out there?

The thing is, if there is *a world out there*, would a teenager know that world existed anymore? "A 2018 Pew Research Center survey of nearly seven hundred and fifty 13-to 17-year-olds found that 45% are online almost constantly, and 97% use a social media platform, such as YouTube, Facebook, Instagram or Snapchat."[8]

That's almost half of all teenagers literally *living* their precious, young, beautiful lives ONLINE! Think of it, two eyeballs staring hour after hour at a screen, instead of utilizing their five senses in this great, blue marble of a wonderful, exciting world of ours! If that is you, you have probably forgotten by now that you have five senses. Seeing, smelling, hearing, tasting, and of course, touching and feeling! You are operating only with your sense of sight!

The "good" of social media

The "good" of social media can be:

- Creation of an online identity (This could go onto both the good and bad lists). An online identity which reflects the *real* you *might* be a good thing, however, when you aren't actually being *you*, how good can THAT be?

- Positive, Supportive, Kind, Empathetic Interaction with others.

- Social networking, as in you like bees and I like bees, or you like Scrabble and I like Scrabble, or you like Ed Sheeran and I like Ed, too. Or you need help with math, and I am great at math. Social networking was meant to be a positive experience.

- Entertainment is limitless.

- Controlled Self-Anonymous Expression.

- Keep up on current happenings around town and elsewhere in the world, like they actually found ice-water crystal balls on the moon! Exciting things like that make the social media a great place when it is used wisely and efficiently.

- World-wide interaction.

- A plethora of information about anything you want to know more about.

- Can be fun and distracting.

- For some, it establishes meaningful relationships with peers, as long as there is a user time limit.

The bad & ugly of social media

Social Media is a relatively "new" phenomenon; however, most teenagers can't remember a time when there was not *social media*. Scientists and physicians are just beginning to study what reaction the Internet is creating in human beings, especially young human beings like teenagers. There are at least 800 million documents on the World Wide Web, which was created in the 1980s. The Internet, as you know it now, was born on January 1, 1983. Of course, it has gone through many changes from its original TCP/IP protocol. A 2019 study ". . . of more than 6,500 twelve-to fifteen-year-olds in the United States found that those who spent more than three hours a day using social media might be at heightened risk for mental health problems. Another 2019 study of more than 12,000 thirteen-to sixteen-year-olds in England found that using social media more than three times a day predicted poor mental health and well-being in teens."[9]

What does this mean to you, a teenager, with a strong dandelion mindset?

Generally, it means that you must control you and your own utilization of the Internet. You can't wait for *someone* else to control you and restrict your use. You must form a mindset which protects YOURSELF. It won't be easy, but it CAN be done!

There is a real world "out there" that you should and can explore on a regular basis.

Teenagers can no longer just blame Covid, as bad as it was, for their depression symptoms. *Who wouldn't get depressed only using one of their five senses for months on end?*

Are you over-using the Internet? Check off these clues:

Personal Symptoms to be on the lookout for:

- Depression. (And no one in your life has passed away, including gerbils!)

- Anxiety. (Are you nail biting, overeating, undereating, jittery, fearful?)

- Upset when you can't log on. (Like to the point of major anxiety!)

- Bad sleep quality—always tired but locked into the screen with those eyeballs!

- Invalid comparisons to other teenagers, like everyone has a better life, better clothes, better shoes, better car, more friends, better food, more "likes" than you do.

- Negative feedback from others affecting personal life/health. *Are you the boss of you and in control of yourself, or does that mean-spirited person make choices for YOU?* Hey, get real. (Remember the dandelion that gets crushed by the boot? Resilience! No one crushes you!)

- Less joy in life in general—thinking everyone else is happier than you are, based on Internet content such as Facebook, Tweets, etc.

- Improper sexual encounters: sharing of intimate photos (Remember boundaries)

- Being bullied by others, or bullying others. (You might feel unhappy, but when you reach out and hurt others to make yourself feel better is becoming a bully yourself.)

- Being harassed/blackmailed due to releasing too much personal information.

Is the situation hopeless? Are you helpless?

Of course, the situation is not hopeless, and of course, you are definitely not helpless! You are a resilient teenager with your own mind. You might even be a trendsetter. When a friend says, "Let's chat online after school," you might be inclined to say, "Meet me at the skating rink or skate park," or "Let's go for a bike ride."

Time for a "Grandma Yarn" about the "old days"

First of all, the "old days" were not all good, nor were the old days all bad. There once was a black-and-white cartoon of two birds sitting on a tree branch. One says, "What do you wanna do?" and the other one says, "I dunno, what do you wanna do?", and the two birds keep shrugging their shoulders, and asking the same thing over again. *Why would that cartoon stay fresh in someone's mind over fifty years?* Because it was the lament of all young teens in those days and probably is right now for you. *What to do on a Saturday? What to do on a Friday night?* Teens DO suffer from boredom if they don't take charge of their own lives. The thing is, you know you aren't yet old enough to do some things on your own. Sometimes, teenagers *feel* old enough to do certain things, but they aren't truly at the age of knowing the full dangers or problems with experiencing certain things.

Check it out!

Here is a list of activities to choose from which do NOT include using the Internet and require that you do NOT use your phone:

- Join a youth group or the Y, or a church group, and sign up for every single field trip. Why? Because you will never have enough time in this life to explore everything in this world, so you'd better get started! (Hint: You will explore using more than just your two eyeballs.)

- Sign up for EVERY school outing. If there is a bus to a football/basketball/track meet—sign up!

- Go get ice cream with a friend and hang at the ice cream shop and talk—no phones allowed!

- Learn how to: Change the oil in the car. (Get permission first, of course!)

- Practice changing the tire of a car.

- Learn to sail on a lake.

- Join a bike club, or just go on a bike ride.

- Go skateboarding or roller skating.

- Make a kite and go fly it. (You could join a kite flying club.)

- Audition for a play at school or local community theater. (It is not all about just acting. It is about set building, scene painting, costume making, sound booth management, and directing too, among other things.)

- Go fishing. (Lots of life's problems melt away when you are smelling pine trees and watching dragonflies over the water.)

- Play basketball/baseball/football/tennis/ping pong—any sport you like—in the park or after school.

- Volunteer to help others doing something you enjoy or teaching something to others.

- Learn to sword fight (which is called fencing).

- Take a tumbling/trampoline class.

- Get a part-time job. (Dog walking anyone?)

- Join an orienteering club. (Nothing like being dumped out somewhere and using your compass and a map to find your way back—no cellphones!) Create your own orienteering club with some friends.

- Create an obstacle course for bikes/skates or make a zipline.

- Make a tilt-o-wheel out of a wooden box, roller skate wheels, wooden ramps, and rope. (Take turns on the rope, while the other person 'rides' in the box over the ramps.)

- Go camping. (The backyard or park is fine if it is

allowed.)

- Visit a museum/art exhibit/street fair.

- Find a huge tree with big branches and climb it. (Better yet, make a tree fort.)

- Make an obstacle fitness course. (Climbed into a refrigerator box 'tunnel' lately?)

- Learn how to golf, or learn archery, or ride a horse (if it's affordable).

- Go to the zoo. (Read each of the information labels; maybe draw an animal you are watching if you like art or write a story about one of the animals when you get home if you like writing.)

- Ask an older neighbor if they need help with anything.

- Wash the car.

- Take a cooking class.

- Learn to sew or knit or crochet. (Football players have been knitters, just FYI.)

- Add to this list regularly!

· · · ● · ● ● · ·

3

"I See You"

Who are you?

Humans change a lot from infancy to adulthood. Their bodies change, and their minds change. Sometimes, you might start out thinking one thing, but then you experience something which changes your mind. Generally, when someone speaks of a *mindset,* they are speaking of 'focus.' When you keep a solid *mindset,* you are basically focused on what you tend to do or not do. Some *mindsets* change as you get older, but other *mindsets* stay solid throughout your life.

What do you think about yourself?

What you think about yourself matters. Sometimes, others can say hurtful things about you, but if you are of the *mindset* that you know who you are, then no one's negative words can change that. Yet, when we are young, sometimes, we do not realize that we have a right to ask someone to stop saying something negative about us. When you are young, you value the opinions of your parents, your grandparents, other relatives, and some friends. We don't realize that their negative comments can follow us into our adulthood if we let them. You are in control of you, and you have a right to tell someone to stop bullying you or saying mean or hurtful things about you.

Another "Grandma Yarn"

There once was a teenager who was just a normal-looking, normal-sized person. A teen from today might say this person was NOT really 'fire.' This teenager got average grades; nothing to shout great words of joy about but passing grades. Yet, there was a major obstacle this teen had to fight with every single day—a mother at home who said things like, "You will never amount to anything. You are so lazy. Look how you folded that towel. You call that folding? Why don't you stop eating? You need to lose weight. You are never going to find anyone who likes you. Why can't you care more about your appearance . . . your grades . . . your hair . . ." and on and on and on. As a result, this teenager suffered greatly from low self-esteem. Self-esteem is just another word for feeling self-worth or feeling good about yourself. This teen did not feel worthy of anything. This teen did not speak up and tell the mother to stop belittling them. *Why not?* Because this teenager had too much respect for their parents.

Note to teens: Respect goes both ways. This person had to navigate their teen years until becoming an adult thinking they were a lazy, unkept, stupid individual. That type of mindset keeps people from success. That type of mindset keeps people from making goals and achieving them. This teen felt like there was a gigantic "L" on their forehead for "Loser."

However, in the case of THIS particular teenager, the negative comments made them strive even harder in life. They developed a thriving mindset. The high school years were not happy ones, just mostly long lonely days. Grades were just okay because this teenager had no enthusiasm to even try. However, once the light of freedom (sunlight on the dandelion!) shone on this teenager's life, there were straight A's in college and always working in management positions as an adult. The teenager turned the negatives the parent tried to instill in them into positives for their life.

There are undoubtedly negatives in your life. Everyone has negative things that happen or are voiced in their life, but you have the power within you to overcome all of them.

Self-respect

Would it have been right for the teenager to tell the parent to stop putting them down? In retrospect, after a lifetime of building up self-esteem, of facing life's challenges, perhaps the teenager should have asked to sit down to talk to the parent about feelings, and how feelings matter, and how words matter. Yet, some parents are difficult to approach. It is very important for you to realize that you DESERVE to be respected, AND that you also need to respect others.

Self-respect is what will take you through life for the long journey, even over the bumpy times. Make up your mind; *have the mindset* that you deserve respect, and that you will always be respectful to others. No one controls your thoughts about YOU. Yes, teenagers must obey parents, teachers, and society's rules. However, it is VERY important for them to know and internalize that they are worthy of respect, too.

Value who you are

Do you value yourself? Do you value your own opinions? Do you not raise your hand in class and offer your opinion out of fear that someone might laugh? Yes, someone might, but you will not shrivel up and die. You might feel uncomfortable, but remember, all the experiences you have are building a strong character mindset within you. You are building that strong mindset every single day. It is not easy when you are up against the negativity of your peers. But even then, knowing your mindset of valuing who you are will help you to weather any negative comments your peers might make. *Does it still hurt when someone calls you a name or excludes you?* Of course it hurts; you are human, and those feelings of rejection ARE painful and do need to be recognized and felt. However, you are of the *mindset* that you do not give the power of your emotions and feelings into other people's control.

Do you acknowledge and know your gifts?

Do you feel intelligent? Of course, we are not all smart in everything, but we all possess certain *gifts.* Do you know your gifts? If you don't believe you have any *gifts,* you most certainly do! Teenagers need to know what their gifts are—your *gifts* are how you will be able to develop your talents.

Do you *have a way with dogs?* That's a gift of working with animals. Do you know how to teach things in a different way to someone who is confused? Like, do you say to your friend, "I don't do it that way, it's too hard, but here's how I do it." Do you know how to trim roses to produce more flowers? Can you bake great cakes? Are you an artist? Are you great with mechanical things?

There are silly things we learn in our teen years, like how we can hold our breath longer than anyone else or stand on one foot longer. Take all the wins you can in life, but know that, sometimes, when you don't succeed at something, you learn the most from the experience.

Challenges build character.

Building the "Trust Factor"

For others to really SEE you and KNOW you, it is important for you to know yourself.

Unfortunately, sometimes the people around you may chip away at who you really are. There are many reasons for this. When adults constantly chip at their teenager, oftentimes they are seeing traits in you that they want to change because they have those same traits. Maybe THEIR self-esteem is low, so they become a bully themselves. Anyone can become a bully. Sometimes, the person isn't even aware that they are a bully. There isn't much you can do when parents are the bullies. You can voice your opinion, but with some parents that only makes the situation worse. But if a teacher is a bully, you can tell your parents or an administrator about the situation and get help.

Do not suffer in silence. Certainly, NEVER take physical abuse from ANYONE. Seek someone you trust to help you.

People who seem to mean well

Perhaps these people don't mean to chisel away at you, but teachers, parents, friends, churches, and others sometimes say things which influence individuals for their entire lives. Some hurtful things can sting for an entire lifetime—if you let them.

When you know there are other people who grew up and had to push through hurtful things in their youth, just like you are doing, it might make you feel like you can tackle those obstacles, as well. Of course, hearing someone say to you, "Oh, you'll be fine, I went through that," is NOT comforting when you are going through it yourself.

•‍ •‍ •‍ •‍ •‍ •‍ •‍ •‍ •‍ •

4

Lists, Plans & Goals

Be positive!

You are a work in progress. You are still growing. Your body is still changing. No one has to point out the physical changes in your body. You SEE them, and you FEEL them. Some of the changes might annoy you, but acceptance is the key.

There is much to do in your life ahead, and even today! It is very important that you develop and keep a positive mindset about your life's changes. *What does that mean?* It means you will make up your mind to be as happy as you can, but when adversity does strike, your *mindset* will become one of a *can-do attitude* or *acceptance* of what *is*—the 'dandelion' mindset of strength under adversity and change.

Most people can do anything they put their minds to. Be prepared to meet the challenges ahead with your mindset of knowing that you are going to give your all, not because someone else wants your good grades, or someone else has threatened negative consequences if you don't achieve them—be prepared because YOU want to be successful for YOU! You want the ability to choose your future, and you know that with hard work and diligence and a strong positive mindset, you will arrive at your destination.

Part of having a positive mindset is acceptance.

Be practical

Lists and plans or objectives can help keep you on track to achieve your plans and goals. Begin to envision how you want your life to be when you are an adult. This will keep you moving toward a growth mindset. When you can envision a future, you can develop the steps to get there. (Some people make a vision board.)

NO fear of failure

Experiencing failure is one of the steppingstones towards your growth. Without failure there is no movement toward success. Actually, the word 'failure' has such a negative connotation, when in reality it is validation that one has tried one's best; validation that steps were taken to do what needed to be done. And if the goal has still not been achieved, you can examine all the steps you went through, and see what could have been done differently to get a different outcome.

Role models

On your quest to reach goals and move through objectives, who can help you stay on track? Who can help you negotiate the many challenges that arise in life? Many teenagers look to famous singers and movie stars as their role models.

This often sets a teenager up for failure because these high-profile people often have many emotional issues, which are magnified by media coverage. These high-profile role models *are* people—people who have been fortunate in their lives. Some of these people do not stop to think how much they influence others, but remember, they are just people. They experience happiness, sadness, and challenges, just like you. They can also make bad choices in their lives, but millions of people are watching!

Picking your role model

This is a fairly important task. You should make choosing your role model one of your top priorities. A role model is so important because that role model can become your mentor—someone who assists you in reaching your goals. Sometimes, we don't actually *choose* our role model—it just kind of happens. A person comes along who just naturally is there for you. This person provides the inspiration and support you need to succeed in reaching your objectives and your ultimate goals. In the "old days," parents picked out godparents for their children. These godparents were supposed to guide the child throughout life, watch over them, and basically, give the child ideas on how to have a good life. Sometimes godparents trained the child in a specific career. Most teenagers do not use their godparents as their role models. In fact, some teens don't even know who their godparents are or even if they have any.

Who could you seek out to be a good role model? Where can you find a mentor in your life journey?

Grandma's "Yarn Time"

There once was a teenager who was a little bit introverted, meaning this teenager kept to herself, and perhaps wasn't comfortable around a lot of people. Her home life was a bit wild and wooly. Her parents argued a lot about money matters—not having enough. Divorce was always *on the table*. The teenager could not talk things over with her parents; they were too busy dealing with their own problems. She became closer and closer to her drama teacher. He was a man from another country, which the girl found intriguing. He always pushed her to do more in his drama class. He wanted her to write more plays, direct more plays, and act in more shows than other students. He believed in her abilities. He insisted that she learn how to build sets and work in the sound booth. Not once did she think he pushed too much. She wanted to succeed, she wanted to please him! He was her mentor.

The drama teacher believed in her so much that she began to believe in herself. He took one of her plays to a university for review, and the university raved about it. She was shocked. Fifty years later, she would look for this professor because she wanted to thank him. She wanted to thank him for sparking the desire to achieve, the mindset to keep going, no matter what was going on in her life, or her family life. He was the reason she went on to teach drama and volunteer to direct children's community theater. He was the one who ensured she went on to college to get a Bachelor of Science degree, and later, a master's degree in education. He was the mentor and role model who changed her life. A mentor and role model can help you focus on your very important life!

Moral of the story: You need to find a role model who will help keep you on track to achieve your goals. Also, if a teacher is particularly supportive of you, thank them! When this teenager went to find and thank this professor, he had passed on.

Along life's way, let people know you appreciate them.

What can a good role model do for you?[10]

- A good role model can help you achieve your passions

- A good role model will help you believe in yourself

- A good role model will give you their opinions when you ask for them

- A good role model will provide emotional support to let you know you are never alone

- A good role model will help you explore school choices and career choices

- A good role model takes care of themselves physically and emotionally—giving you a good example to do the same

Dad or Grandpa as a role model

Don't laugh. Yes, Dad can be goofy at times, and Grandpa seems like he is on mind trips now and again, but both of these men have experienced life as young boys. They have had their share of successes and failures and have a wealth of information. Ask them to share it with you. Ask them meaningful questions about their youth. For teenagers who don't have a dad or grandpa active in their life, an uncle or a coach can be a good role model too.

Mom or Grandma as a role model

Did Mom do anything shady when she was your age? Would she share with you some of her failures and successes? Does Grandma have any pointers about her time as a cheerleader or track runner? Did Grandma march for Civil Rights? You'd be surprised at the nuggets of information and helpful hints you could glean from Grandma or your mom. Take the time to ask. Take the time to listen to their answers.

Familiarity with your role model

You may or may not meet your favorite football player, or your favorite actress. You might want to be just like them. You might want to follow the exact path to stardom they followed. However, role models are like guides in life. They share their life stories. They share their wisdom, as they try to keep you from going through the same setbacks. It is better to model your life, if you choose to do that, with someone close to you, someone in your daily circle of life. Pastors, coaches, teachers, or relatives are all generally good role model choices.

• • • •• • ◉ • • •

5

WAITING, WANTING, WORRYING...

Are you waiting for others to love you?

Are you wanting love and worrying about love? You are not alone having those feelings. 75% of teens in the United States become seriously involved in romantic relationships in their quest for finding someone to love them.[11] Worldwide, 35% of teens have dated and are in some type of romantic involvement due to them seeking and needing love.

Why is this so important to you, beyond having someone to love and who loves you in return?

Teen love helps build resiliency for later on in your life. In this sense, being "in" love when you are a teenager is not a 'bad' thing. Yet the reality is that 64% of teens are in the waiting, wanting, and worrying stage of finding love, just like you may be.

Waiting for love

There's plenty of time for romantic love, but of course, millions of songs have been written about young love. Teenagers sometimes become impatient waiting for it—but true love is worth the wait. For sure, you have heard that before so many times, however, now is the time to internalize that knowledge. True love has so many facets that go far beyond just the emotional involvement. In the end, true love is more about the other person's needs than about yourself and your wants and needs.

Wanting love

Everyone wants to BE loved. This is a human trait, as discussed before. It is more than just wanting to be touched and cared for. You want someone to share the laughter with you, the moments in life that are precious to you. But also, when you are feeling out of sorts and down, you want someone to be 'there' for you, in essence, to *catch you if you fall* or to *watch your back*.

Worrying about love

As a teenager, you have many deep concerns, but the greatest of them is about how you will cope with all the changes in your life, in your body, and yes, if you find someone who will love you—just for you. Worrying is just another name for 'anxiety.' Anxiety can come in many forms, cold sweaty palms, jitters, or an uneasy feeling in the pit of your stomach.

When worry equals severe anxiety

There are times when you must tell your parents/caregivers or your doctor about your anxiety. If you find the following situations apply to you, get some professional help, or at the very least, speak to them, or another trustworthy adult, like a school counselor, about it. Do not try to conquer your anxiety or worrying by yourself.

- You are having panic attacks

- You are avoiding your family or your friends, or social events and situations

- You are having stomach aches or headaches frequently

- You are tempted to "try" some substance to make you feel less anxious or stressed

- You feel constantly sad or depressed

Can reading this book help you 'find' love?

Actually, honestly, maybe.

If you change your focus on to YOU—new and wonderful things can begin to happen.

It is like a crazy "magnet principle." When you feel like you are all right, that you matter, that your opinions matter, and you feel you are in control of yourself and your life, others can see that confidence and are attracted to it.

Why are people attracted to confident individuals?

Confidence breeds confidence, meaning that when you are with someone who tells you, "You can do it!", you honestly feel you have support and that you can do whatever is challenging you. This is why many teenagers move through their life in groups or packs, because they feed on each other's confidence. Most teenagers feel exactly like you do. They are anxious about things in their lives, too. They may not show it, they may not tell anyone, but going through the teen years has some similarities for everyone. Teenagers are on the edge of growing up, and standing on that edge of adulthood can be daunting at times. Teenagers generally don't want to "stick out," they want to "blend in."

The questions you may ask yourself

- Am I dressed right?

- Is my hair okay?

- Did I do my homework correctly?

- Will people laugh at my report when I read it in class?

- Will someone ask me to dance at the dance?

- Should I ask someone to dance at the dance?

- Am I too thin?

- Will I get my driver's license?

- Am I too fat?

- Will they notice my pimple?

The questions that trigger anxiety go on and on . . .

Time for a "Grandma Yarn"

Teenage girls and boys have tons of these types of questions and feelings. There once was a fourteen-year-old young fellow who wanted to ask a girl to a dance at school. He had his eye on her for some time, and he really thought she was pretty. (Always remember that Shakespeare was correct when he wrote (even though he was probably quoting Plato at the time): 'Beauty is in the eye of the beholder." *What does that phrase mean?*

Well, it means that others see your beauty or handsomeness when they look at you. Some of us may like brown hair or black hair or brown eyes, but what we like, we see as beauty. Anyhow, the boy was finally ready to ask the girl to the dance. He was going to do it at lunch break at school. He practiced exactly how he would ask her. It was only three days away before he would meet her at lunch and ask.

Well, as fate would have it, or let's just say a teenager's luck, on the third day when he woke up and looked in the mirror, he had a gigantic pimple forming on the END of his nose! It was one of those big, red, bulbous, gigantic kind that hurt when you touch them. The kind of pimple that *shows* up when you are nervous but want to look your best. Now . . . what to do? *What would you do?* Would you give up?

He did not give up. He spoke to his mother about what make-up is best to cover blemishes. Yes, his mother helped him cover the pimple, though it was still there and still big, it was no longer red. He asked the girl to the dance, but his first words were, "Try not to look at the bulb on the end of my nose." They both ended up laughing. She even told him about a time when she'd had one of those type of pimples on her chin.

Bravery often pays off. In fact, most of the time, a person can make up stories of exaggerated fears in their own head which can ultimately defeat their aims.

This young man found a solution because he refused to just give up, even when the universe seemed to be aligned against him.

- Do you keep moving forward, no matter what?

- Do you look for solutions, instead of being defeated?

Did you know that boys are more romantic than girls?

Who knew, right? Generally, teenagers fall hard and deeply in love, even when that love might not be a 'good' love for them. This young love is so important that it sets a person up for a future of the same type of love experiences, whether or not they are good for the person or not.

So, can you protect yourself from getting entangled in unhealthy relationships?

Love is a powerful "glue" that is right up there with the Gorilla-type brand glues, both when you are young and, believe it or not, even when you are older. Minimizing mistakes from the beginning is a strategy which makes sense for all people contemplating love. There is no minimizing feelings of love. A five-year-old's love can be as intense as an 80-year-old's love. When a human being falls in love, it is always epic. When a teenager falls in love, it is real, and it is intense.

Ways to minimize risks of love

- Make thoughtful decisions about falling in love

- Refuse *unwanted* love gestures (whether it is holding hands or a kiss, or more)

- Keep your own mindset; do not give over your own personal control to another person—no matter how much you love them!

- Avoid partners who want to manipulate you or control you

Quality friendships

Friendship is very important to you at this time of your life. Finding friends is sometimes not as easy as one might think.

Where do you look for a friend?

- Seek friends who share your interests

- Seek friends who come from the same background as you

- Seek friends at the gym/football field/skating rink/dance class/newspaper club/book club—anywhere you frequently visit

- Seek friends in your classes

- Seek friends at the Boys & Girls Club

- Seek friends at your place of worship

Focus on *you* and *your* needs

At first, it may sound a bit selfish, focusing on yourself, but these are the years where you will be making some major decisions which can affect your entire life. You are at the center of all your decisions.

You might even hear your parents saying, "Enjoy these years," because they remember how quickly they go by!

School years

Sixth, seventh, and eighth grade really whizz by. It is all so overwhelming! No one seems to understand you or what you want to do, or where you want to go. You have all these *feelings*, and they all seem to be hitting you at once—anger, happiness, insecurity, and yes, love! Every time you want to assert your independence, it feels like *someone* is holding you back. Maybe your parents, teachers, or sometimes, even yourself! You can and should begin to make some decisions for yourself.

Let's cut through the seriousness!

Yes, you do have to keep up with your schoolwork and your grades. That's a given.

Look for things you can enjoy which will take some of that seriousness away and give you a chance to laugh and to breathe.

 Join in extracurricular activities: During these school years, many young teens back off from sports, yet keeping up at least one sport, especially team sports, is great for building solid friendships that can last for years. If your passion lies elsewhere, you might perhaps try writing for the school newspaper, or join a debate team, or why not try out for a part in a play? You may have to force yourself into activities, but it can only be worthwhile!

 College is important, yes, but right now, if you study, and do your homework, you are doing your part. Try not to worry so much about something that is so far away. Steady as you go! Do what you are supposed to do, and that will take care of the future.

 Release the pressure hanging over your head to choose "what you want to be when you grow up." Instead, use these teen years to do lots of investigations. Try many things. Explore. Volunteer. It is natural to want to be a botanist while you are studying plants in science, but when you take that engineer prep class, you want to become a mechanic. These are the years of exploration! Enjoy!

 Go play with your friends. Don't let "play" be a thing of the past. Don't think you are 'too old to play.' Go roller blading, play baseball or softball, go skateboarding, sailing, hiking, video gaming, cooking, play board games, ping pong, or just hang with your friends. Laugh a lot. Don't try to solve all your life plans by the time you are 15!

Games

Here's a fun game to try. Sometimes, we feel like our world around us is like hot lava, and we are miserable and don't know where to turn. This game lets the players move and jump and laugh. It takes a little prepping, but when you have a small group of friends, you can play it in the garage or a large family room. If you play it in the park, you can declare things which are "safe" to run to.

"The Ground is Lava!" game

Prepping: If there are 5 players, make 5 different colors of "rocks." Using large sheets of construction paper in five different colors works fine. Use three of each color, so you have 15 "rocks." You will also need some strong removable tape to tape the "rocks" to the floor in various places. You will need to make a spinner with the same 5 colors on it. To play the game, the MC hollers, "The ground is lava!" and spins and announces the safe color, i.e., "green!" Everyone must try to avoid touching the lava and jump to a "safe" green "rock." If you play this game outdoors, instead of using a spinner, you can have the "MC" or "caller" announce, "Only things that are blue are safe," or "only things you can sit on are safe." People can run to blue things, or, in the second example, to benches, chairs etc. Eventually, some people will not be able to move, and they are "out." You keep playing until there is a winner, or you can have two winners, first and second place.

Love words of warning

Remember the dandelion and how lovers pluck the petals as a type of game, asking if one is loved or not? Like the hot lava in the game, becoming too involved before you are ready can spell hardship in many ways. One important way is when falling IN love becomes such a huge distraction that everything else falls by the wayside.

Grandma's "Yarn Time"

Oh, we were all young and in love at one time or another, but there was a fella, a tall, lanky boy, with brown curly hair and big, brown, sad, doe-deer eyes, who fell in love. He was fourteen and an only child. He had lots of love in his life and in his world, so he wasn't *starved for love* like some young people are, but that didn't mean he wouldn't be bitten by that love bug when it came around! If you've been stung by the love bug, you know exactly how it feels. The young man loved this person more than anyone in the whole world. She was his poetic morning, noon, and night. She was his sun, moon, and stars. Okay, so you understand this wasn't just a light love; this was duck-hunting, wader-boots-deep love. Love notes; Texts; Nights of long conversations until the wee hours; Finding himself sleepy in class because they'd stayed up too late talking on the phone. (He loved it when first period at school showed a movie so he could sleep.) Sharing music; Sharing their soda; Sharing their food; Sharing their dreams; Spending their time totally, completely wrapped up in each other. You have the 'picture' now, right?

Shocker!

Well, the love of his life suddenly left him and moved away. In an instant, his sun, moon, and stars were gone! Now what? He collapsed into tears, he couldn't eat for days, and no one in his entire family could console him. He felt like this was the end of his life. The parents ended up calling the grandma, who drove three hours to come and comfort her grandson.

How did the grandma do that?

The Grandma brought the fifteen-year-old a teddy bear to hug.

He didn't say a word. He unwrapped that teddy bear, tears rolled down his face, and he ran away up the stairs with Teddy clutched in his arms. *Would his friends ever know?* Only if HE told them.

What is the moral of "Grandma's Yarn" this time?

Yes, we all need love, and we are NEVER too old to hug a teddy bear . . . jus' sayin' . . .

Adults vs teen feelings

When adults try to minimize the feelings of young people, they do teenagers a grave dis-service. The adults have obviously forgotten how important and intense feelings can be when one is young. Teen love is as real as love at any age. Sometimes, it is even more intense than love at other ages.

• • • ● • ● • • • •

6

KNOW YOUR GIFTS

Here's one way to identify your gifts. Ask yourself these three questions.[12]

1. What task can I do that I am best at, where I don't even have to try?

2. What do other people say about me all the time as my 'gift'?

3. How can I use it, or how have I utilized it in my life so far?

Remember that a 'gift' is not a 'talent.' A talent is something you work hard at to try to learn how to do and perfect, like playing the guitar. A gift is a wonderful type of actual part of you which comes naturally from your birth. Some examples of gifts are:

- Creative mind—always thinking up stories/ideas or writing music

- People are drawn to you and feel comfortable around you

- Mathematical mind—seeing things analytically naturally

- A voice that is naturally melodious for beautiful singing

- Ability to "see the big picture"

- Ability to "see the small picture"

- Ability to calm others during life's storms

- Out-going personality

- Ability to listen to others

- Communicate well and effortlessly with others

- Drawing, painting, artistic/designing ability

- Ability to always know the right questions to ask

- Ability to have patience

What is an "inner voice"?

This is you speaking silently to you. This "inner voice" happens within your own brain. You silently might say, "No, don't do this," or "This is great, do it!" Your inner voice often tells you how much *you* mean to *you*. That may sound strange to read, but if your inner voice says to you, "You are worthless," then you can come to believe your inner voice. Or if your inner voice says, "You can do it!", you come to believe in yourself.

You can work to change your inner voice, which basically represents your silent thoughts. When a negative thought pops in, immediately replace it with a positive thought!

Gifts and your inner voice

When you know you have a gift, you can listen to your inner thoughts as to how you can best utilize it to develop certain talents based on your gift. You can use your gifts to propel you into a prosperous, happy future. For example, if your "gift" includes having a naturally mathematical, analytical mind, then what type of career paths might interest you? In a sense, by knowing your gifts, you can begin to rewire your mind for success toward goals that fit your gifts. A school counselor can give you a quiz that identifies your gifts and strengths, to help you zero-in on what talents you should try to develop, and which careers might be a good path for you.

Don't be pigeon-holed!

What does being 'pigeon-holed' mean? It means being labeled as something, put in a box, so that avenues are blocked off to developing possible new skills, learning new knowledge, and not being open to new challenges or different directions and goals. Sometimes, this happens, for example, when a parent is guiding your career choices instead of you. If Mom or Dad is a doctor, perhaps they want you to become a doctor, too, and everything they do and say is guiding you toward that goal. Maybe your parents want you to "take over their business" and are pushing you to follow that path.

Solution—the art of compromise!

Sit down with your parents/caregivers/teacher/ counselor and talk to them about your strengths and your talents—and of course, your gifts. *Will this be easy?* Probably not. Sometimes, it is difficult for a teenager to do a serious face-to-face talk with their parents/caregivers when there is disagreement. But it must be done when your dreams are clashing with their ideas for your future.

Parents are generally wise

Yes, parents are older and generally wise about the ways of the world, and you should listen to them. However, respecting your desire for growth in the way you want to go is also important for them to understand. Try using this verbal technique: "Yes, I know you want the best for me, and I respect that. I know you have more experience in the ways of the world. However, I have the gift of playing music, which I would like to pursue parallel to my formal education, if that would be all right with you. I do not want to waste my gift." If you are talented in music and want to go off and create a band, tell them so. Also, reassure them that you will keep up your grades in all other areas, as well. Let them know you understand their concerns, and that you will continue to do well academically, while also pursuing your 'gift' and developing your musical talent.

Your mental attitude is the key

Your willingness to share your thoughts and ideas with your parents/caregivers and your ability to attempt to 'see' their viewpoint, will go a long way in paving a smoother road for you. Mental Attitude is the key to success, actually, in all your teen endeavors. Try to let go of the mindset that "everyone is trying to control me." Adopt the mindset that others are "trying to help me make wise choices." When you become angry, you stunt your ability to see things clearly and set yourself up for more stress and fewer solutions. Your mindset needs to be one of openness for growth.

Growth is not always easy and, sometimes, it can be even a bit painful.

Becoming grateful

This is a fast-paced world you live in, but when you pause to be grateful for the gifts you have been given, and the talents which you have learned, something very positive develops within you. It is easier to smile. It is easier to let go of the stress of everyday life.

Sometimes, we think our life is absolutely horrible, until we 'see' the life of another. We may find ourselves wishing we were taller, or have brown eyes, or have the build for a football player, and on and on. Be grateful for *you* just as you are this moment in time. Love yourself. Be grateful for your parents. Be grateful for your family. Be grateful for your friends. If being grateful is difficult for you, think of one thing, just one, that you are grateful for. It can be the alarm clock that gets you out of bed in the morning, or that cup of coffee. Learn to practice gratitude.

Time for a "Grandma Yarn"

True story time again. There once was a boy who griped nonstop to his parents that he did not like his nose. He didn't like the shape of his nose, the length of his nose, absolutely nothing about his nose made him happy. He told his parents that the size of his nose was making him self-conscious, and that as soon as he was an adult, he would get a new nose. He wanted plastic surgery on his nose. Then, one day he was standing in line at a burger place, and he turned to look at the man behind him in line. The man had no nose. He had two holes to breathe through, but no nose! The boy politely turned back in line and said nothing, but that young man never again wished his nose was any different. He is now a man in his 70s, but he has never forgotten that man in line without a nose. He was instantly grateful for his own face *with* his nose from that moment on.

Moral of the story: We should be grateful for what we have and what gifts we have been given. It is up to us what we do with our gifts and talents, but we also must appreciate the person we are, the body we live in. We are all different, and our outer body-shell is different from those of others. Learning to look inside yourself for your gifts and developing those gifts into great talents, rather than wasting time and energy on thinking "I wish I could look like him/her," or "If I just had that ____ (fill in the blank with your wish), I would be successful." Appreciating what we **do** have and then taking the challenges headfirst with a "can do" mindset moves you forward to where you want to go. Complaining and grumping about what you don't have, or what you can't have, stunts your growth and makes you spin your proverbial 'wheels' in the mud. **Acceptance** is a big part of maturity.

How can you break through barriers to a positive mindset?

First, get your mind in the right place. Yes, unpleasant things can and do happen in everyone's lives, but if you start with a positive mindset, there will be nothing you cannot work through. This is where your positive self-talk mindset comes in big time! Sometimes, it means you must talk yourself through something. For example, if you have a math test ahead of you and math is not your strongest subject, begin to talk to yourself about what you need to do to pass the test. Don't look outside yourself for someone else to *make* you study. Give yourself permission to not be perfect, but also, be determined to pass—and begin to study as soon as you know when the test date is. Self-talk yourself by saying, "I can do this. I can pass this test." Your mindset should be one where you know you can do it, with the proper preparation.

Many teenagers wait for the external "hammer" to fall before they take hold of their own lives. They might even say things like, "My dad is gonna have a fit over this report card." The person who should really be upset is YOU. Your dad already had a series of his own report cards; he wants a better life for you.

The *pushing and shoving* to do better should be coming from YOU. This is your life! Those are your grades. The future is your future! Sometimes, it helps to be reminded of that.

Mindset goals & priorities

Who sets your priorities in life?

YOU. Yes, your parents can be nagging you from the sidelines, to "Study!" or "Get better grades," but who is the one person on earth who can accomplish that? Yep—you. Get out of the mindset where you rely on parents or caregivers to "make" you do something. This is YOUR life, and the future will be YOUR life. You will either prepare yourself for it, or you won't.

Isn't it time for you to have a *mindset of success*?

People who succeed at reaching their goals and have their dreams come true push themselves to do what is necessary for success.

Isn't it time for you to realize that only YOU can set your priorities? Yes, at seven years old, your parents had to set a little clock and told you to do your homework—or they didn't, and you did it on your own, or you didn't. But now, you are a teenager, and you are responsible for *you* and your own actions AND, most importantly, your future success.

Try on different "hats"

You may not remember, but when you were in kindergarten you might have tried on different dress-up clothes of people in different careers: the hat of a firefighter, the cape of an actor, the eyeglasses of a teacher, the helmet of a football player, a construction worker's hard-hat and boots, the tall, white hat of a baker, or the apron of a butcher. It is just as important now for you to try on different 'hats,' though not literally, like you did in kindergarten! It is time for you to investigate possible future paths which you might like to pursue.

No matter which "hat"—have a positive mindset

Try not to just cross careers off your list saying, "Oh, I can't do that; I am lousy at biology." Instead, keep a positive mindset and utilize positive self-talk. Say to yourself, "I wonder if I could take a few classes in biology to see if I like it and I can learn it." Do not cut yourself off from future possibilities without thinking deeply about them first. Be open!

A word to the wise—In life, it isn't always about the Grade Point Average. Yes, grades ARE important. However, if allowed, take a difficult class as a pass/fail. Give yourself the ability to just explore and learn a new subject without being too concerned about the grade. Take a class because you know nothing about it and just want to learn more about the something.

• • • ● • ● • • •

7

LASSO TOXIC FEELINGS

If you are constantly looking back at things that happened to you in the past, or you are constantly looking at what you think are your short comings, you are not going to be able to move forward with success in your life. Toxic feelings can hold you back from happiness and success. How can you change the world if you are preoccupied with a past which you cannot change?

Get up on that horse again!

It is so important that when you have a setback in your life, at any stage, like a low grade on a test, or that person you like won't go out with you, or your parents won't let you have a car or driver's license yet, try to accept certain things as being "just the way it is" for now.

Get back up on your horse and keep riding forward. Lasso any toxic feelings of anger or disappointment and acknowledge your feelings as real. However, do not let your feelings hold you back from moving forward! Make a positive plan and follow it.

What are toxic feelings?

Toxic feelings are no more than emotions such as being sad, or having anger, or experiencing fear that you do not express and gradually become damaging to your wellbeing and confidence. If you establish some strategies to cope with these negative, often draining feelings PRIOR to when you have them, you will be prepared to *head them off at the pass.* (That's an Old American West idiom that lawmen used to say when they were going to catch the bad guys just in case you were wondering.)

• • • ● ● • ● ● • • •

8

CONTROL YOUR MINDSET

Take a step back and let yourself feel whatever you are feeling. Be mindful of exactly what you are feeling. Don't deny your feelings. *Feel* them. Sometimes, these feelings hurt, but they need to be acknowledged. Use your self-talk to say, "It is okay to feel what I am feeling. I feel so hurt and so angry," or express whatever you are feeling. Then, tell yourself, "I know I can cope with this, even though it hurts so much."

Remember, YOU must care for you. You will be with you for the rest of your life. Most people don't pause to take in that reality. Sometimes, you need special care, so do something you know will soothe you. *Will a bath or shower calm your nerves? Will a walk in the park, breathing fresh air, help ground your emotions again?* Whatever you must do to console yourself that is healthy, do it. Maybe you could get a haircut or go shopping or go to a movie and let yourself get carried away in the story.

Get a piece of paper and write down the positive aspects in your life. Look deeply with a heart of gratitude for the things and people you have in your life. (Remember the man with the nose if it helps, just to bring your gratitude into focus.)

After doing the above, get outside yourself: Go help someone else. Nothing gets us out of our own misery more than reaching out to help others. Maybe volunteer at a food kitchen, tutor someone at school in a subject you are strong in, offer to walk someone's dog, or perhaps offer to run an errand for someone who is ill.

Call a friend you trust, or if you feel comfortable, speak with your parents or another adult you trust. Ask for advice. Ask for help. Asking for help is often difficult to do, but sometimes, you can be overwhelmed by what you are feeling. You will be surprised to find out that others have experienced what you are going through. Share your feelings, your thoughts, and your worries, and you will likely get a supportive response.

If your toxic feelings don't begin to abate, if you find yourself carrying them everywhere with you in a heavy sack of misery, perhaps you need to seek a professional to help you through this toxic time. Professionals are trained to give you tools to work through various problems in life. A professional can help you help yourself.

A mindset for success

For some teenagers, it is a waiting 'game.' They wait and wait for someone else to care about them, or someone else to tell them they must do their schoolwork or else this or that will happen, but that is NOT a mindset for success.

- Success is grabbing your own life with both fists and facing all the challenges head-on.

- Success is doing what is required to pass a class in

school.

- Success is having the 'maturity' to ask for help when you need it.

  ○ Ask a friend who knows how to do a problem for help after class.

  ○ Ask the teacher for a meeting so they can explain the problem to you, to help you understand it better

  ○ Go see a counselor at school for help in getting an easier class, or harder class, or a different class. Don't wait!

- Success is beginning to focus on career ideas/choices:

  ○ Speak to your parents/caregivers/teachers about careers

  ○ Speak to the school counselor about career choices to use your natural gifts and develop your talents

  ○ Begin to read or watch movies about different careers

- Success is knowing when to play and when to be serious.

- Success is acting with intention and purpose.

• • • ● • ● • ● • •

9

THE MEDIA CIRCUS

What do you think about 'media time limits' for teenagers?

The suggestion by "experts" is that anyone under eighteen should not have more than sixty minutes per day of media usage. In the "old days," like circa the 1960s, people imagined the future with humans having gigantic heads because they didn't utilize their extremities, which atrophied (withered) over time. Young people imagined that evolution would take over like it had with many species, and humans would consist of mainly a very large head and tinier, weaker arms and legs! (Are you imagining that 'new' human right now?)

Do you think their futuristic image is far off?

Have human heads grown disproportionately? Well, since 1825 to 1985 human heads have, on average, grown a third of an inch! One could argue, 'Well, that's super, more room for thoughts and knowledge.' But are humans slowly becoming all heads and no bodies? That's a bit of *food for thought* when one begins to think about teenagers spending eight hours a day in front of a computer screen. Human bodies were meant to move, to run, to use their arm and leg muscles—not just their minds.

Are the new rules of TikTok saving us from ourselves?

It comes back to self-preservation and you taking care of you. *Do you think you could or would regulate your own time on the media circus bandwagon?*

Ask yourself these questions:

- Am I balancing my life with physical activity—like sports?

- Am I finishing my homework and school projects on time?

- Am I spending time with my family, or am I grumpy if I have to?

- Am I spending time with my friends which doesn't include playing video games?

- Have I been gaining weight because I snack in front of the screen?

- Do I have problems paying attention to my teachers or my parents?

- Do I go to sleep easily at night and stay asleep?

• Am I irritable at home or school?

Answering these questions honestly can help you to identify and realize if you are spending too much time staring at a computer screen instead of living your life in the "real world."

The computer world

Anyone can say they are anyone on the Internet. They can say they are a whizz at jumping hurdles; they can say they are first in their class at math computation; they can say they are six feet tall and have big muscles when they don't at all; they can say they are 22 years old when they are thirteen years old; they can say they are fifteen when they are really sixty; they can say they have long, shiny hair to their waist when they are bald; they can say they live at the beach or in a city when they live somewhere else entirely. Basically, people on the Internet can say whatever others will believe.

The computer world of "friends" is NOT the real world. No matter how *real* it feels. Perhaps it might be time for you to cut your time in the fantasy world to a shorter time period and go out into the 'real world' to have a 'real life.' Yes, life is sometimes hard, but isn't high-fiving your friend for real better than just clicking a high five emoticon on your phone or computer? Isn't successfully cutting your time running the track every day more of a personal accomplishment than shooting ten more zombies in a video game?

Yes, real life takes real commitment and involvement. Yes, you will have to motivate yourself (and maybe a friend or two) to turn off the games, turn off the computers, to get out of the chat rooms. No one can truly "make" you do that—only you can, by being mindful of you, your future, and your own mental health. Parents/caregivers can set boundaries, but you know if you don't want to do it, you will find a way around it.

The only way you will succeed is IF you want to change the trajectory of your own life to pursue a more successful, happier future. You are in control of you.

Making a conscious effort to change is working on a new mindset!

Change is not easy for humans. We are kind of like a bronco horse not wanting a saddle on its back. Most humans—at any age—do not like to change what makes them feel good. But sometimes, feeling *good* is not the same thing as being healthy and strong.

Sometimes in life, you will have to just choose to do *what is right.*

• • • ● • ● • • •

10

PARENTS/CAREGIVERS HELP CORNER

Just because they are your parents and caregivers does not mean they *magically* have all the answers on how they can help you achieve a positive mindset to seek your best life possible. True, up to when you were a certain age, they were your superheroes. They might still be your superheroes, which would be a wonderful thing, but most teens begin to see that their parents and caregivers do the best they can, but those adults who guide you aren't magicians.

Actually, parents or caregivers are another set of 'tools' which a teenager has in their life's toolbox to help them. Yet, the bottom line is that they are just human, like you. No one gave them a manual on *How to Raise the Best Human Being Possible*. Most parents wing it. (You know about *winging it*, right? That's when you don't study for a test, and you just take a chance you know the information—*you wing it!*)

Baby books

Almost everyone expecting a baby buys a 'baby' book, to help them know what their baby looks like at every stage of pregnancy. Sometimes, prospective parents buy "how to" parent-type books. Every parent can use a little help once their child reaches their teens. Books like *Brainstorm: The Power and Purpose of the Teenage Brain* by Daniel Siegal, *Untangled: Guiding Teenage Girls Through 7 Transitions* by Lisa Damour, and *The Book You Wish Your Parents Had Read* by Phillippa Perry can give some insight on how to parent a teenager.

Actually, reading *this* book can give parents and caregivers insight into how to help teens become all they are meant to become in life.

A parent/caregiver of a teenager can't be their child's best buddy

Do you think of your parents as your best friends? If that is true, it can be both a good and a not-so-good thing. Remember, parents must say "no" to you sometimes, and they must make rules to keep you safe. The 'no' might bother you, and the rules might irritate you, and you might get a bit perturbed about your "friends" having the audacity to tell you "no"—which causes major conflict.

Parents and caregivers are NOT supposed to be your friends. They are adults responsible for your safety and wellbeing. Maybe later, say, when you are 25 and they are in their 50s, friendship is warranted. But not now, not when they are guiding you through the murky waters of your teen years. You need to have a solid anchor through these times of questions and indecision. You need boundaries and, of course, should face consequences if you break through those boundaries. That is not a job for a 'friend.' Parents, caregivers, teachers, coaches, clergy, and any adult in any position of power, are all supposed to be role models for youth. They are the "lighthouse" that keeps shining its light so that a teenager is never left alone in the dark.

A quick note to parents, tucked in among all these wise words

Dear Parents/Caregivers,

Just a note to remind you that you are NOT your teenager's best

friend. It is great if you get along well, but you are the people whose job is to be the "lighthouse" for your child. You are who your teenager

will be looking to for guidance during difficult times. You are the ones

whom your teenager will want to set boundaries, to keep them safe.

Here are some key points to remember:[13]

- Research video games and screentime shows before your teen watches them to regulate content.

- Encourage your teenager to play sports like tennis, ping pong, golf, football, basketball, swimming, dancing, aerobics, etc.

- No screen watching at mealtimes.

- No screens in bedrooms, including TV.

- Screen time should be earned when homework and chores are done.

- Feel free to block what you do not want your child to view online. Put safety locks online wherever you feel there is a need to. You are the parent.

- Keep computers in a common family area so that you know what is going on.

- Teach your child the dangers of the Internet. Talk to them about sexting and sharing information and photos. Knowledge is power, and safety.

- Enjoy sharing some of their time with them online.

- Set an amount of time your child can be online. 60 minutes per day has been made as a suggestion. Work with your teen to see what works for everyone involved.

Life's curve balls

"In life, we need to have an acceptance of *what is*. It can be hard to let go of the past and to accept whatever event happened to us. The more we fight instead of having an acceptance of what is, the more likely we are to suffer and experience pain. Life will always throw curve balls we can't prepare for or anticipate . . ."[14]

What are the things a person must accept in life?

1. Accept yourself. Accept who you are, how you look,

what are your good parts, what you perceive as not so good—accept your gifts and your short comings. Just embrace "YOU." Be good to you!

2. Nothing ever stays the same. Life is always in a state of flux. Places change. People change. Ideas about things change. What you believe at fifteen you may not believe at twenty.

3. Accept that you will age. You will not be sixteen again, nor thirteen. You will always be "Daddy's girl" or "Mama's boy" to your parents, but you are beginning to think for yourself and beginning to establish your own mindset. Most importantly, as far as we currently know, you cannot relive an age. Yes, it is a case of "YOLO," but it should be lived well, not destructively. Parents can't relive their childhoods by borrowing yours, either. This is your time to be a teenager, not theirs! Sometimes, teens yell at their parents in anger "This is MY life!" The thing is, yes, it IS your life, so take charge and do right by yourself.

4. Try not to be morbid and accept that in life, we sometimes lose people, even pets, that we care about. While your family and friends are here, let them know you care about them. Hug them whenever you can. Tell them what you think of them and why.

5. There is no true order. If you continually try to get on a bandstand and control your entire life, you will fail. There is NO controlling life. It is random and full of chaos. You plan to go to a baseball game, and it gets rained out. You fall in love with a girl, and she falls in love with someone else! You buy the unique gift for your best friend, and someone gives him the

same thing. The best plans can get waylaid. This can create sadness and stress for people who plan out their entire lives. Yes, you need to plan for your education and a future career, but you also need to be open to possibilities along the way. Parents need to realize that the little bundle in their arms at birth will have its own mind and its own dreams, especially by the time that infant is a teenager.

6. You are not your thoughts, and you are not someone else's thoughts about you, either.[15] If someone has told you mean and hurtful things, like "you are so stupid," or "you will never amount to anything," or "you can't do anything right," just know, you are not *their* thoughts either. Be mindful of your thoughts. If you begin to hear negative thoughts in your mind, immediately change them. You have the ability to "play a different track" in your own head. Replace the negative thought with a positive one.
Parents, be mindful of your words because that teenager of yours will remember your words FOREVER. Your teenager isn't a baby anymore; your teenager has the ability to remember the hurt and the pain caused by words.

7. People have their own minds and mindsets. You can never control people. We can lead by example, which is fine, but we cannot make them follow any certain path in life. Sometimes, people won't like you, and that's okay. Sometimes, people will love you, and that's a wonderful thing. Acceptance will mean that you do not have to be sad because everyone doesn't care for you or like you. You are a great person. You know it, and that must be enough sometimes.

8. Family is family. You can't change that. You can pick friends and treat them like family, but family will always be "blood."

Family that plays together, stays together?

Yes, your parents and you have different ideas, and your thoughts about certain things might not align. But when you play a game together as a family, all those differences somehow wash away.

How about playing a family game with those "blood" relatives of yours?

There are many games to purchase which offer fun for families and, at the same time, open the channels for communication. One such game is "How Well Do You Really Know Your Family?" It costs about twenty-five dollars to buy, but you can modify the original game to play without having to buy it. Simply have everyone write down five things about themselves on a slip of paper. Everyone puts the answers in a hat. The game involves picking a paper at random in turn and trying to work out from the answers which family member wrote what. You can have five set questions to write down, for instance, a favorite color, favorite food, favorite restaurant with the family, favorite book or movie, or say, the best place the family ever visited together. So, if the answer given is *blue is my favorite color*, the question is, *who wrote that blue is their favorite color?* Everyone writes down what they think is the right answer. Those who get it right get a point. Game point could be whoever gets to ten points first. The five questions for everyone to answer can be changed each time you play.

Family game of "Spoons"

You will need:

- 1 deck of cards, shuffled.

- There should be a spoon for every player but one, placed in a long line in the middle of the table—there are not enough spoons for everyone—you are always one short!

Deal everyone 4 cards.

Game starts with passing one card to the left.

Once you have 4 of a kind, yell "spoons!", while grabbing for a spoon.

The one without a spoon is the loser and gets awarded the first letter of spoons, an "S."

Once anyone spells "Spoons" in its entirety, they are out of the game.

Everyone is to pass the cards swiftly, putting them in the front of each player, but a player can only pass one card to the left each time. Sometimes, a player is slow and the pile in front of them gets bigger, but they still can only pass one at a time.

Continue the game but remove one spoon again, and so on.

This game is fun and noisy! The purpose is just to get the family to interact together and to laugh and enjoy being together.

Families are made up of individuals

You might not like everyone in your family, and perhaps someone doesn't care for you much, either, but that does NOT mean you cannot all sit down and play a game together or have a meal together. Learning tolerance for each other is a necessary part of life.

Human tolerance of others

Humans must try to tolerate other people's mindsets, even if they are different from their own. Each person has a right to their own mindset and beliefs without fear of retribution. This goes for EVERYTHING in life.

Tolerance is important. Being tolerant of other people's way of being, their religious beliefs, their way of dressing, their way of speaking, their mindset, or their thoughts on different subjects makes for a more peaceful world. As long as you tolerate others and they tolerate you, and you don't interfere with their lives, and they don't interfere with yours—there is peaceful co-existence. The only time humans get into murky waters is when a person believes others MUST believe or act as they believe and act.

One last "Grandma's Yarn"

This is for you, Teenagers, and also for your parents and caregivers.

Keep in mind that the "teen years" are only six years long. Sometimes, people act as if the teen years go on to infinity, but nope, six short years: Age thirteen to nineteen.

Parents will reflect on how quickly that newborn baby went off to first grade. That's how long these teen years are, but the years seem to go by much more quickly, for some reason. Teenagers and parents/caregivers can have a wonderful six years, or it can be six years wrought with tears, pain, anger, or fear.

It is your choice.

The teen's choice.

The parents'/caregivers' choice.

The story

There once was a parent who had three children. In the teen years, all three of the children had unique issues they had to work through. Of course, we all know that no two people are exactly alike; even twins have their differences. These three teen siblings were no different.

One, a daughter, experimented with alcohol, which caused the young teen a lot of sadness and misery. Often teens think parents are being overbearing when they mandate rules such as "no substance use," but in the end, it is most often to help their teenager avoid heartaches. The daughter was the head rifle brigade coach at high school, but she fell off the stage inebriated from alcohol at a school cheer camp. That meant she not only had to go home immediately, and her parent had to come and pick her up, but she also lost the three-foot-high gold trophy she had won and worked so hard for.

Teen experiences can linger a lifetime if you let them. She never quite got over that loss for about twenty years. She was an adult with her own children, still remembering the feeling of loss. *Can parents stop their teenagers from experiencing this type of pain?* Generally, and sadly, no. Some things in life teenagers just have to deal with and learn about on their own.

One of the sons decided he would go joyriding in his parents' new car—which resulted in a car crash that almost took his life. Thankfully, he survived the crash into the large, brick mailbox. He was so embarrassed and ashamed. His parents were just grateful he was alive, but to him, he felt like a failure and a disappointment. He spent years trying to get back his 'polished' reputation of the 'good son.'

The other son kept fighting the family rules; he bucked curfew, and ended up being sent to a special, tough academic school, and he still swears to this day that the time away at that school changed his life for the better. He is now forty years old and has told many parents to send their teens to the same international school. He says it was a privilege to have attended along with international students from all over the world, and that the experience changed his life only for the better.

Three different people

Those three teenagers came from a good home, with hardworking parents who paid attention to their lives. There were football games, dances, driving to dates, all the things that parents do to try to make their teenagers' lives better and happier. But the thing is, as was said previously, it is what it is. The parents could not completely protect their children from themselves and their own teen choices. Your parents will try to protect you, too, but only you will be making the choices.

It is important for teens and their parents to realize that all kinds of storms of life can come at you at times, really hurtful and painful times, but you will make it through.

Why will you be able to make it through the storms of life?

You make up your mind to be strong and to believe that things will be all right. You develop a mindset of strength. Life has a way of righting itself when you are patient. Make up your mind to be strong and to face life head-on. Don't hide. Don't run.

Yet, remember, the storms DO pass. Also remember, you are not alone in this world, and that every single person has had their share of "life storms." Seek out someone to anchor you in the times of your storms—your parents/caregivers, close friends, grandparents, relatives, a coach, or a teacher.

Mindset

The word "mindset" means just that—set your mind to steady yourself, no matter what life brings your way. *Will it get tough sometimes?* You bet it will, but you can handle whatever comes your way with a mindset of success and a mindset that says tough times are a part of life, too. Your mindset should also be that it is okay to ask for help, in fact, it is very important that you recognize when you do need help and ASK for it.

Success

The three teenagers grew up to have beautiful families of their own, and between the three of them, they have nine children. When teens and parents go through certain situations, it can seem like the end of the world sometimes. There is a temptation to give up, but with a *mindset for success,* there is nothing to stop you from moving through the difficult times with a clear head and finding solutions.

Will you always be successful?

Hopefully, yes, but logically, not always. But always aim for success and believe in yourself. Plan to succeed, but also accept that sometimes plans must change.

Enjoy your teen years.

Have a mindset of joy, and you WILL be joyful!

Have a mindset of anticipation for good things to happen, and good things WILL happen!

Have a mindset that YOU will enjoy your teen years by not doing anything to yourself or making choices which sabotage your happiness.

You are ultimately in control of you.

You are in the driver's seat of your life.

When you know this and understand it, resentment toward your parents/caregivers, teachers, or others in authority will not bother you.

These people are only in your life to support you and guide you.

You will be making ALL the choices—good choices and bad choices.

Keep your heart light. Be happy!

Make a wish and blow the dandelion seeds to your heart's content, and always have a dream.

The compass of your life

Write down your goals and the objectives needed to meet them.

Your goals will change often, and so will your objectives, but your goals will become the compass of your life.

Your goals guide you to learn new things, practice new things, do new things.

Your goals push you to become whatever and whomever you want to become.

Your positive mindset is the guide to your healthy happy life!

Postscript to "Grandma's Yarn"

All three of those teenagers became successful in owning their own businesses and following their distinctly different dreams. They had three unique, distinct paths, but their mindset was always to succeed!

So—they did!

And you will too!

Always keep a *Mindset of Success!*

• • • • • • • • • •

ABOUT THE AUTHOR

Ariana Smith is a financial expert, entrepreneur, and writer. Her many years of professional and personal experience through motherhood have nurtured in her a passion for telling inspiring stories to children, teens, and young adults.

She is passionate about empowering young readers to embrace their own identities. Ariana believes in instilling timeless values through history and literature; her mission is to help young generations find their purpose and develop self-confidence and skills that will help them lead fulfilling lives doing what they love.

Ariana's books are written in simple and engaging language and can be read independently by children, teens, or their parents. Her work has proved especially valuable to young readers seeking to develop critical thinking skills.

When she's not writing, you will find Ariana reading, cooking, or spending time with her beloved husband and their three beautiful children.

Visit Ariana's website to learn more. Sign-up to her newsletter to stay connected and get her upcoming books for free!

www.ariana-smith.com

READ MORE

Inspiring career guides for teenage girls and boys including tips and exercises that will prepare them for the future.

READ MORE

An unmissable collection of detailed biographies and important stories about successful women for teens and young adults.

REFERENCES

Bennett, Jessica. "How to Clean Your Bedroom in an Hour for a More Restful Space." November 21, 2022. bhg.com/homekeeping/house-cleaning/tips/quick-clean-bedroom/

BeSophro. Blog: "Why are Role Models So Important for Our Youth?" be-sophro.com/blog/why-are-role-models-so-important-for-our-youth/

Brenner, Grant Hilary, MD, DFAPA. "The 5 Kinds of Teen Love." ExperiMentations. December 26, 2022. psychologytoday.com/us/blog/experimentations/202212/the-landscape-of-teen-love

Brown, Robert. *World Economic Forum.* "Top Ten Jobs of the Future—2030 And Beyond." May 18, 2021. weforum.org/agenda/2021/05/jobs-of-the-future-year-2030/

Campbell, Alison. Parent Influence: *Toxic Parents: These Posts Prove That Some People Should Never Become Parents.* parentinfluence.com/some-people-should-never-become-parents-is/

Cherry, Kendra. *What is Resilience?* March 13, 2023.
verywellmind.com/what-is-resilience-2795059

Dou, Tina. "Learn About What is Empathy—3 Types of
Empathy." Acuity Insights. June 24, 2020.
acuityinsights.app/2020/06/empathy-1/

Fielding, Sarah. Mental Health News. Verywellmind. "TikTok
Put 60 Minute Daily Time Limits on People Under 18—Should
We All Do It?" March 26, 2023.
verywellmind.com/should-everyone-limit-their-social-media-
use-7368887

Harvey, Steve. "3 Key Questions that Will Help You Identify
Your Gift." 2023 Steve Harvey Global.
steveharvey.com/3-key-questions-that-will-help-you-
identify-your-gift/

Johns Hopkins Children's Hospital. "Screen Time Guidelines
for Teens." 2023.
hopkinsallchildrens.org/Patients-Families/Health-
Library/HealthDocNew/Screen-Time-Guidelines-for-Teens

Kellogg, Kristi. *Teen Vogue.* "171 Best "Never Have I Ever
Questions That Dig Deep." December 22, 2022.
teenvogue.com/story/never-have-i-ever-questions

Lamoreau, Karen; Litner, Jennifer; Sharkey, Lauren. "What
Does It Mean to Be Touch Starved?" Medically reviewed.
April 8, 2021.
healthline.com/health/touch-starved

Larkin, Claire. Babbel Magazine. "What is Culture Shock and
How Can you Avoid it?" March 23, 2018.

babbel.com/en/magazine/what-is-culture-shock

Magnolya, Ziva and Ryan, Stacey. 2022. 'Fall in Love Alone.' Recorded by Stacey and Ziva on Best of 2022 Album December 16, 2022. Record Label UME Clearing House.

Mayo Clinic Staff. "Tween and Teen Health." *Teens and Social Media Use, What's the Impact?* February 26, 2022. mayoclinic.org/healthy-lifestyle/tween-and-teen-health/in-depth/teens-and-social-media-use/art-20474437

Mayo Clinic Staff. "Positive Thinking. Stop Negative Self-Talk to Reduce Stress." Stress Management. February 23, 2022. mayoclinic.org/healthy-lifestyle/stress-management/in-depth /positive-thinking/art-20043950

Medium. "How to Survive Toxic Feelings and Emotional Hangovers." April 2023. medium.com/@infinitepassion/how-to-survive-toxic-feelings - and-emotional-hangovers-7d5ffaa46381

Miller, Caroline. "How Anxiety Affects Teenagers." Child Mind Institute. childmind.org/article/signs-of-anxiety-in-teenagers/

Morin, Amy, LCSW. VeryWell. "10 Social Issues and Problems that Trouble Today's Teens." September 20, 2022. verywellfamily.com/startling-facts-about-todays-teenagers-2608914

Morin, Amy, LCSW. VeryWell. "How to Talk to Your Teen About Friendship." February 7, 2022. verywellfamily.com/talking-to-teens-about-friendship-2610992

Mosher, Dave. National Geographic News. June 8, 2012.

nationalgeographic.com/culture/article/120606-americans-heads-getting-bigger-science-health-skulls-evolution

Online Library Learning. A Historical Reference. usg.edu/galileo/skills/unit07/internet07_07.phtml

Oxford University Press. languages.oup.com/google-dictionary-en/

Pew Research Center. "Teens, Technology, and Romantic Relationships." October 1, 2015. pewresearch.org/internet/2015/10/01/basics-of-teen-romantic -relationships

Rogol AD. Emotional Deprivation in Children: Growth Faltering and *Reversible* Hypopituitarism. Front Endocrinol (Lausanne). 2020 Oct 7;11:596144. doi: 10.3389/fendo.2020.596144. PMID: 33117295; PMCID: PMC7575787. ncbi.nlm.nih.gov/pmc/articles/PMC7575787/

Ruth B. "Dandelions". Album *Safe Haven*. 2017. Columbia Records. "Wishing on dandelions."

Sealey, Lindsay. *Tiny Beans Voice Contributor.* "Preparing Teens for the Future." April 22, 2020. tinybeans.com/planning-preparing-teen-girls-for-the-future/

Sharpe, Rachel. Declutter the Mind. "Acceptance of What Is: 17 Things to Accept in Life." January 11, 2022. declutterthemind.com/blog/acceptance/

Sidhu, Ranjit. ChangeQuest. "Change in Management." January 11, 2022. changequest.co.uk/blog/7-steps-to-prepare-for-change-changequest/

Slack Team. By the Team at Slack. February 19, 2019.
slack.com/blog/collaboration/psychological-safety-building-trust-teams

Smart, Collett. Host. 2023 April 20. "?The Importance of Touch." *Raising Teens podcast, Relationships.* Spotify. S1, Ep 05 *The Importance of Touch.*
raisingteenagers.com.au/the-importance-of-touch/

Steane, Richard. BioTopics.co.uk.
biotopics.co.uk/genes1/bodypartcloning.html

Walter, Phil. "The Truth Behind Eskimo Kisses." March 12, 2019.
curioushistorian.com/the-truth-behind-eskimo-kisses

Wikipedia contributors. (2022, November 21). Let There Be Peace on Earth (song).
en.wikipedia.org/w/index.php?title=Let_There_Be_Peace_on_ Earth_(song)&oldid=1123001590

1. Steane, Richard. BioTopics.co.uk.

2. Smart, Collett. Host. 2023 April 20. "The Importance of Touch". Raising Teens podcast, Relationships. Spotify. S1, Ep 05 The Importance of Touch.

3. Wikipedia contributors. (2022, November 21). Let There Be Peace on Earth (song). In Wikipedia, The Free Encyclopedia.

4. Magnolya, Ziva and Ryan, Stacey. 2022. 'Fall in Love Alone.' Recorded by Stacey and Ziva on Best of 2022 Album December 16, 2022. Record Label UME Clearing House.

5. Dou, Tina. "Learn About What is Empathy—3 Types of Empathy." Acuity Insights. June 24, 2020.

6. Lamoreau, Karen; Litner, Jennifer; Sharkey, Lauren. "What Does It Mean to Be Touch Starved?" Medically reviewed. April 8, 2021.

7. Larkin, Claire. Babbel Magazine. "What is Culture Shock and How Can you Avoid it?" March 23, 2018.

8. Mayo Clinic Staff. "Tween and Teen Health." Teens and Social Media Use, What's the Impact? February 26, 2022.

9. Ibid

10. BeSophro. "Why are Role Models So Important for Our Youth?" Retrieved April 5, 2023.

11. Brenner, Grant Hilary, MD, DFAPA. "The 5 Kinds of Teen Love". ExperiMentations. December 26, 2022.

12. Harvey, Steve. "3 Key Questions that Will Help You Identify Your Gift." 2023 Steve Harvey Global.

13. Johns Hopkins Children's Hospital. "Screen Time Guidelines for Teens." 2023.

14. Sharpe, Rachel. Declutter the Mind. "Acceptance of What Is: 17 Things to Accept in Life." January 11, 2022.

15. Ibid

Made in United States
Orlando, FL
30 November 2024

54670666R00065